I VOTE . . .
And I Hate Politicians

I VOTE . . .
And I Hate Politicians

John D. Good

Library of Congress Control Number:		2010916524
ISBN:	Hardcover	978-1-4568-0984-3
	Softcover	978-1-4568-0983-6
	eBook	978-1-4568-0985-0

To order additional copies of this book, contact:
Xlibris LLC
1-888-795-4274
www.Xlibris.com
Orders@Xlibris.com
589657

Contents

Preface..7

Chapter 1: The Problem 27

Chapter 2: Freedom Of Speech...38

Chapter 3: The Solution...43

Chapter 4: A Time For Change Is Now....................................58

Chapter 5: Cleanup On Aisle 4...... 60

Chapter 6: How This Will Not Work 64

Chapter 7: Oversight? Oversight!
            I Don't Havta Provide No Stinkin' Oversight!..................68

Chapter 8: Let's Get Started 72

Prologue...81

About The Author 85

Preface

I truly believe there is inherent good in all human beings on this planet. It certainly starts that way from the day we are born, but then as we mature and our beliefs and core values, taught to us early in life, become increasingly challenged. Notably in our adolescent years, we all want to be liked and received into the popular groups while finding some commonality with our way of thinking as our piers begin to show their support by accepting us in. Then as we mature and are able to internalize the difference between right and wrong and what is perceived as mainstream beliefs, we become somewhat disillusioned and uncertain which direction to go. As I mentioned above, we all start out believing in the good in other people due to one simple trait and that is trust. When we trust that another person will protect us and not challenge this bond we have developed together, then we never question their actions even if they unintentionally violate that connection that drew us together and kept us together. When someone becomes mentally or physically abusive towards another person, or simply ignores them, the victim in this case so wants to find justification in the action of that person they have this strong attachment with so they can continue that level of trust, love and respect they have grown to believe in. It is because we learn early on about right and wrong but rarely seem to be able to internalize between good and evil that conflicting attitudes and beliefs constantly challenge our core beliefs throughout our lifetime. Because of this, good people are taken advantage of, manipulated, and brainwashed into acting out what they are lead to believe is the way of the majority and certainly what the populace is in favor of doing. One way to assure you are not lead down a path you may regret later in life is to take control of your own destiny and trust that your personal core values and intuition will always guide your conscience in the right direction.

Case in point is the ever increasing number of restrictions placed on women seeking medical treatment essential to their health and well being. Why would any woman support diminished health care that they or someone they know may need at some point in their lives? Especially when all the restrictions placed on a woman's right to choose their own personal health options, are levied against them by men! Think about it women, who knows more about your own physiological makeup than you yourself. Or maybe you see some credence with the claim, by some old white guy, that restricting a woman's right to seek an abortion after being raped is no longer her own personal choice. Because that is classified as a "legitimate rape" with the female body having ways of shutting down the whole birthing process naturally, abortion becomes a non-issue in this person's view. When a woman seeks an abortion after being assaulted, she is really the only one who knows what change is happening with her own body, so I would question, then where does the whole non-issue enter into the picture? If you are a pro-life advocate then it is your personal right to believe as you wish, but you have no right to force your belief system on another person if they choose a different course of action necessary for their own health and well being! Pro-life advocates are waging a deliberate attack against the Equal Rights Amendment to the US Constitution and clearly trying to further diminish the rights of women in this country through their deceitful campaigns. If I were you, I would wise up women because what's coming next could be a law drafted by men for your return to a role in which serving the needs of family come first and foremost, while keeping your opinion on what's best for you to yourself!

As stated above, early on in our lives it is almost instinctual to want to believe and do what is popular and 'happening' with the in crowd, to put it in more outdated terms. The masters of manipulation know where the weaknesses are in others and use that to promote their self-serving campaigns for advancement into positions of power by instilling the fear of some negative outcome should anyone question their baseless and unsubstantiated rhetoric. This is why attorneys make such good politicians. They know how to act out emotional scenarios in order to convince the jury that the person being tried in a court of law is either innocent or guilty of a crime, regardless of the actual truth in the case. If you look at the politicians not driven to fulfill their own self interests but rather are truly advocating for change by helping those citizens most in need of some assistance, such as Senators Bernie Sanders, Sherrod Brown or Rep. Emanuel Cleaver, their previous professions were not in the legal field. President Obama is one of those exceptions as someone who chose to leave the legal profession and enter into public office to try and make a difference through the passage of laws benefitting the majority of citizens in this country over a career of manipulating existing laws only to benefit his firm and their clients.

Most Americans today know that our legislative body of government is broken and would like to see some positive changes to a once respected institution of government, but most citizens feel helpless or overwhelmed and exhausted living day to day to try and do anything about it. That is why we keep electing representatives to go to Washington and try and make changes in *our* best interests. Even though over the past twenty years as best as I can remember, those claiming to have all our backs if elected into public office, have consistently forgotten who their true allegiance is with once they assume their positions of power. So why do people think this next election cycle will be any different? As a matter of fact not only do politicians today not keep the promises to their constituents as they advertised, but more often than not lawmakers have gone rogue in the performance of duties they swore to uphold honestly and ethically when sworn into office. I'm not sure about other voters but I am finding myself with severe 'buyers remorse' today due to the many negative attributes coming to light from candidates I voted for in the past. With the overall approval rating of Congress at 7% today, I'm thinking I may have a few more of my fellow citizens in agreement with me on this.

Unfortunately, the only option voters have today is to wait until the next election cycle and choose the better of the two unqualified candidates who all promise ideal changes to a dysfunctional government and in the end, seem to come down with cases of amnesia once in office. So much precious time has already been wasted by those in power who have neither the urgency nor the ambition to do anything for their fellow Americans! Without even politicizing what members of Congress actually believe in, simply ask yourselves which of the individuals currently in office have ever done anything to improve the quality of life for you or your family personally. Does anyone really think mostly the male millionaire members in Congress could care less about finding solutions with the inequities so many good citizens are facing today in our society? Of course not. These wealthy members of Congress are bored with their personal lives while continually looking for some excitement and the sense of power achieved by their purposefully ruining the lives and livelihoods of so many innocent people in return. We continue to hold out hope that this time a candidate will enter office devoted to carrying out the message they promised voters to deliver on. Unfortunately, one person's message cannot guarantee change in the minds of others with differing beliefs and ideals. One person's code of ethics and societal values that get them though their life on a daily basis is certainly not a generic belief system that one should assume would work for others as it seems to for you individually. Never forget that it is each and everyone's right to live and practice their own personal beliefs in this country as long as they respect that same private and personal right for others to hold for themselves.

The people of this great nation have but one option remaining and that is by voting to stop the true madness currently seen in Congress due to a select group of unscrupulous operatives. Later in the book I propose a way to hold those lawmakers accountable for the unprecedented dysfunction they have intentionally created in today's legislative branch of government. Then, after we start to right the sinking ship in Washington, I believe there is a way to alleviate this current stigma, seen with our dysfunctional leadership in government, by people around the world, and to never have it taint our nations image again. I therefore urge everyone eligible to vote to please do so starting in the upcoming election this November. Our choices in this and elections following are still going to be limited until we decide to hit the restart button with the whole process. Until then please realize that the outcome through our current process can have lasting and possible harmful effects on current and future generations if we do not vote our conscience this time instead of trying to indoctrinate others with our own personal beliefs and voiced by the masters of deceit and deception running for office.

Personally, I have never before seen a once giving and caring society in which I grew up in, transformed into today's contrasting environment of hate and discontent towards other living creatures simply because people have differing views and beliefs. For whatever reason you may dislike the progressive agenda or dislike what the president represents to you personally, the fact is voting to have the GOP control the Senate and the House is fruitless, as long as Barack Obama, our current president remains to complete his second term in office. Contrary to what the minority leader in the Senate feels his power over the president may be, Barack Obama still holds veto power over any legislation voted for by the majority in Congress and exercises that privilege if he feels bills are not in the best interest of all Americans prior to signing them into law. Put your ideals and principals aside for the next two years, vote your conscience, and let President Obama complete the promises he made to all Americans in 2008 and 2012. He got the *majority* of popular votes in both elections because the *majority* of people in this country want him to succeed in fulfilling his campaign promises to make America a better place to live for every person in this country. Remember you cannot criticize something until it is tried and put into practice. If the minimum wage is raised for all workers by this administration and we see significant job losses over the next two years as claimed by the naysayers out there, then in 2016 vote for a conservative president and policy makers to further your personal ideals and views because that progressive idea did not work in your opinion. If the idea did not succeed it won't be because the president was wrong but rather it will fail because those opposing it will do nothing to support the change that has proven successful in the states in which it was already implemented. If it did succeed on a national level and millions of hard working individuals started to finally see some improvement to the quality of life for themselves and their family, maybe the current anxiety levels felt by so many and demonstrated through hate and discontent towards others, would start to turn to hope for Americans and we could then start to see positive change with peoples attitudes around the country. The manifestation of hate and hostility towards our fellow citizens has becomes so prevalent in this country today, it now remains a slippery slope for future generations to try and live free and prosper as we so enjoyed in past generations.

Or you can continue to look narrowly at what serves your own best interests first and foremost by sticking to your principals and following the lead of naysayers who continue to promote fear of the unknown as an excuse for inaction. Let's focus on another two years with lawmakers standing on their own personal principals while continuing to draw huge paychecks for doing absolutely nothing, all under the guise of doing their jobs in the best interest of their constituents. I hope you are one of the few beneficiaries of the status quo mentality in Washington, continuing to carry the torch for those making promises they never intend to keep once in office while personally being able to maintain a clear conscience in the future due to your misguided allegiances.

If we as a society are to accept Congress' new role as one for entertainment purposes only then we need to start electing more lawmakers like the Mayor of Toronto since he is at least fun to watch at work. Our lawmakers need a new playbook if they are to continue their current script based on 'adolescents gone wild.' Even during the summer doldrums with reruns on TV, the continuing and dehumanizing antics being carried out with some in Congress are no longer entertaining to the majority of Americans. People today seem to be more energized around a weather phenomenon destroying cities or a commercial airlines being blown out of the sky with significant loss of lives rather than seeing what counterproductive non-issue lawmakers are rallying support among themselves for. That is a telling state of affairs with the mental capacity of people today being unable to absorb any more superfluous commentary, especially when centered around politics.

So let's focus for a moment on the difference between debating an idea and implementing that idea into practice. Many scholar's and specialists in their fields of expertise understand the importance of a collaborative discussion when presenting the pros and cons of an idea before it is implemented and put into practice. Unless some individuals present in the debate have physic powers to see into the future, the final outcome of an idea can only truly be determined once implemented and put to the test in a real-time environment. I personally have accomplished so much in my life already, not by speculating what if, but rather doing and trying what if. Mistakes will be made when acting on an idea for the first time but the real mistake in life is not even trying something because of fear of failure with the ultimate outcome. Lessons learned throughout my journey so far have always reinforced my self-esteem and purpose in life because I weighed success and failure equally. My knowledge base continued to be strengthened as my confidence in the ability to succeed at what ever I undertook grew even stronger with each challenge I met. Bottom line is at least I tried things to see if they were right for me and those around me, while always confident in my ability to fulfill my own personal expectations and more often than not, exceeding them. Challenging my curiosity into practices was far more rewarding than just engaging with the chorus of naysayers while chanting how bad an idea is before ever even tried. I remember once in summer camp, my Cub Scout leader was afraid to go into the woods because he heard wild animals lived in there. What that told me even back then was that our scout leader was afraid of the unknown since no reports were ever released to my knowledge about someone being attacked by wild animals in those woods. If there were, I doubt that event would have published on the list of things to do while at camp. I realized then that another persons fears or convictions should never influence my thinking just because they alone had reservations about doing something they themselves were fearful of.

I think we should all live and practice the following mantra: **Our time on this planet is short. Life is not promised, tomorrow may not come**. Even if we don't face any major financial setbacks and remain in relatively good health, we have at most, 50 years of *quality time* as adults. During this period, life has to have some purpose or meaning. The most gratifying and fulfilling purpose to your life on this planet should be genuinely caring for the well being of others as well as yourself. As long as you have a positive impact on another human while living or after you're gone, your purpose on this planet has been, or will be fulfilled. I know I will never forget those who have touched my emotions and connected with my soul during my life so far. Unfortunately with each new generation this connection and ability to genuinely care for another human being becomes more distant as people and societies of self interests overcome the needs and wants of everyone else. Perhaps because people have experienced so much pain and suffering personally or because of the number of tragedies covered by the news media on a daily basis, our senses have become dulled as we find ourselves today feeling less compassionate with the needs of our neighbors. I grew up during a period in the history of our country where a human being sincerely cared about the well being of another living creature on this planet. People would show their compassion by going out of their way to help those less fortunate first while for the most part accepting responsibility for the outcome of their actions.

I think some news media outlets today by promoting their commentary of fear and hatred toward others around us simply because people have different views and beliefs, have falsely created an atmosphere in this country of distrust towards our fellow citizens. I know it will never go back to the way it was but do you really want your children and grandchildren to live their lives under a belief to "do unto others, before they do unto you," or should we as a society try and advocate now and for future generations to live a more rewarding existence during the brief journey on this planet by "doing unto others as you would have them do unto you." I have often wondered what some of the commentators seen on conservative news shows today discuss with their children or grandchildren about family and societal values. Do these innocent youths know that those who they look up to and trust for their contribution towards a compassionate and caring environment for them to grow up in, are directly responsible for the continued decay of moral values seen around the world today through their negative and hateful commentary. It is obviously important to many conservatives with finding fault in others, so to distract the focus away from their own shortcomings while accepting no responsibility for the humanitarian damage to our entire society that they are contributing to through their toxic dialogue.

I may not agree with everything the president has done while in office thus far, but I certainly cannot validate someone else's claims that *everything* Barack Obama stands for is evil and contrary to the beliefs of the majority of Americans. Conservative news outlets have not even given the president an honorable mention for trying to do the right thing for all Americans. Why is the idea of providing affordable health care *insurance* for everyone in this country such an evil thought to have? Or increasing the minimum wage so more people can work and have a better quality of life to show for it? Or creating jobs by improving much needed infrastructure repairs across the country? Or providing care and shelter for the migrant children coming into this country as a compassionate and humanitarian gesture first while discussing ways to curb the inflow of more illegal's entering our country later on? The presidents' ideas are not evil or counter to mainstream beliefs as some make them out to sound, but rather compassionate and thoughtful ideals that the majority of American's voted him into office for 2 terms in support of his living up to those promises made to us all.

Some people spend their entire existence on this planet seeking the meaning to life. Philosophers expound their beliefs while theologians preach from ancient manuscripts, the message of their savior. Few people are able to internalize their own beliefs or whether they even exist on this planet for a reason. If a person is never able to like themselves or feel good about themselves, then they will never have the capacity to like or love someone else. And how sad that is. People more and more have resorted to establishing their own superficial boundaries of what it means to love someone else or feel compassion for another living being. Of course not being a specialist in the field, I can only speak about this based on my own personal experiences and have no psychological data to support any of the ideas or thoughts presented in this book related to other peoples behavior.

So let's briefly talk politics, the root of all evil surrounding the increasing decay in the moral and societal values seen in this country today. Do you ever ask yourself, when thinking about all the closed door sessions that members of Congress seem to be in, *what are they doing in there?* During a visit to our nations capitol not long ago I thought I would see for myself what goes on behind the scenes with some members of Congress, so I went into the Rayburn House Office Building to poke around the seemingly endless hallways dotted by American flags outside each office. I wanted to see first hand where the most vocal members hung out so I proceeded upstairs to the Gohmert and Bachmann cribs to see how intense a work environment that these dedicated public servants were able to function in, day in and day out. To my surprise even though it was a regular workday for most Americans and this being around 2 pm Eastern Time, staff told me as I stood in the lawmakers reception areas, that they had already left for the day. They then asked me in each of the offices, as if reading from a script, if I was from that members' home state and what party affiliation I voted with. When I did not respond they then asked if I had any message they could relay to the lawmakers for me, if and when they returned. I replied 'no', at which point I exited quickly so staff could return to their regularly scheduled broadcast viewing of Fox News and I could get across the hall to the restroom to relieve myself.

Journalist *John L. O'Sullivan*, wrote an article in 1839 which, while not using the term "Manifest Destiny", did predict a "divine destiny" for the United States based upon values such as equality, rights of conscience, and personal enfranchisement-- "to establish on earth the moral dignity and salvation of man". This destiny was not explicitly territorial, but O'Sullivan predicted that the United States would be one of a "Union of many Republics" sharing those values.

Historian William E. Weeks has noted that three key themes were usually touched upon by advocates of Manifest Destiny:

1. the **virtue** of the American people and their institutions;
2. the **mission** to spread these institutions, thereby redeeming and remaking the world in the image of the U.S.; and
3. the **destiny** under God to accomplish this work.

It is past time to stand up for what our forefathers destined as our unalienable right to live free while demonstrating at all times, compassion for all mankind.

We are approaching six years since President Obama was elected into office and his many achievements continue to be overshadowed by those trying to discredit his administration and his true ambitions with turning the country around from the brink of collapse in 2008, when he came into office. It has been five years of our precious time wasted by having every piece of legislation with the exception of the

Affordable Care Act, drafted to improve most Americans quality of life, opposed by the political obstructionists, showing no sense of urgency to help the most vulnerable citizens in this country. Over a thousand people a day were dying because they were denied healthcare prior to the Affordable Care Act going into effect. Now, at-risk individuals can at least purchase health insurance and see a doctor for treatment and hopefully find some relief from the ailments they may have. Thousands of hard working Americans were loosing their jobs each day just as the previous administration left office in a 'state of chaos'. Currently, the unemployment rate in this nation has fallen below 7%. Corporations are making windfall profits, while the stock market is higher than anytime in the history of America. President Obama has lived up to some of the promises he made to the American people when first entering office in 2008. The President has had to advance this country out of the worst recession since the Great Depression and essentially done so with no support from lawmakers in Congress. Just think where we would be today if he had even some bipartisan support for implementing positive changes through our legislative body of government! How can any rational person condemn an idea until it is actually implemented and put to the test, as was the case with the Affordable Care Act? Ten million people are already praising the positive effect the law has made to their lives by finally being able to seek medical attention that was unavailable to them in the past. Doesn't that statistic make us feel better about change rather than supporting false propaganda campaigns that base their entire claims on fear of the unknown! I know some people are still waiting for those 'death panels' to surface so they can finally say, 'we told you so.' This should be a milestone moment for all American's to rejoice in the fact that no other president in this nations' history has ever been able to achieve such a monumental cause benefiting most Americans as a result. Personally I would like to say, high-five Mr. President!

Going forward we should all unite to take this law to the next level with single-payer health care coverage for every citizen in this great nation. Employers would rejoice if they did not have to administer health insurance plans for their employees, while additionally having the revenue to hire more workers and pay higher wages. Workers would rejoice knowing they would not have to worry about paying for needed health care they have certainly earned and deserve. I have been in countries where socialized medicine not only provides exceptional care to all its citizens but also provides doctors with incentives to actually try and cure patients of those ailments they may have, instead of just prescribing drugs so you will go away and stop complaining all the time. Citizens in those countries are content with their lives because the basic needs of health care, food and shelter are met through government assistance in exchange for their orderly behavior and productive contributions to the societies they live in. Speaking about orderly behavior, what ever happened to that angry Canadian woman who found nothing good about the socialized health care in her country while claiming Obamacare will never work in this country either? Well, the way I see it and the way more people in this country should realize about change, you cannot please everyone all the time, especially if one's displeasure is based solely around an idea instead of an act.

I have come up with a simple thing to say to myself whenever the naysayers criticize an idea that *may* improve my life or someone else's life if allowed to be tried and tested - **They neither have the urgency or the ambition to correct the problem because they themselves are insulated from the crises.** The next time someone says no or 'hell no' to an idea, just apply this simple thought in your mind and their motives will become crystal clear why they are rejecting any change. Speaking of 'hell no,' I have a pet peeve with the talking heads always walking past the podium clamoring 'more jobs' with never even a whisper about more *good jobs*! I don't know about the rest of you but throughout my various career moves, most in high level management positions, the workplace environment where I spent a third of my life, ultimately became an unpleasant place to be for me personally. Every job with the exception of the period of time when I ran my own business, eventually became a toxic environment to work in depending who my boss was at the time. Of course members of Congress never have to worry about an unpleasant work environment because they are either absent from the workplace or accountable to no one while doing nothing when on the job. Truly a **good job** that most of us could only dream of ever having!

Can we put our differences aside for a moment and agree on the fact that Barack Obama is a visionary. Many Americans including myself firmly believe the president is trying to make things right for more of our hard working citizens and those less fortunate who need a helping hand. You are never going to get everyone to agree on change. Change threatens our security and beliefs because it has an unknown outcome. Think for a moment though if we ignore the need for change. Global warming and climate change is a contentious topic these days because although scientific evidence proves global weather patterns are becoming more extreme each year, the cause is still debatable. Heaven forbid Americans would have to consider giving up their ozone destroying SUV's in an effort to save the planet. After all that is not their problem but something for future generations to deal with, if it even becomes an issue during their lifetimes. What is it going to take for people to stop debating the why's and start acting on the fact that extreme, record setting, weather patterns are here and only getting worse. Look back over the past ten years and globally there have been cataclysmic events each and every year, and it's only getting worse. People don't even say their weather conditions this year were the worst they have ever seen since it has now become a reoccurring event year after year. The only reason we are not aggressively promoting alternative energy sources is because the oil industry does not want the competition or loss of market share to solar or wind technology. The campaign to curb the growth of alternative energy sources became evident in Oklahoma recently when the state legislature voted to fine homeowners for choosing alternative energy sources over the local utility provider. I believe that is the same state that is trying to prevent all marriages from taking place since they cannot selectively discriminate with the union between same sex couples! Apparently the green slime craziness out of Washington continues to ooze downhill across the country. Pick your feet up folks because I hear once you get that stuff on you it is hard to clean off as long as the conservative lawmakers are in charge. So ask yourselves, can we wait until the end of days to make a decision to change what we as humans are doing to our planet when the potential for inaction has such severe consequences? It may already be too late for future generations I am afraid.

We the people need to mandate change while demanding our administrators in the government find the most fiscally responsible way to carry out the wishes of the majority of the voters. If the majority of Americans vote to have socialized medicine available to every man woman and child at a certain level of quality care, the governments' responsibility should then be to find the most fiscally responsible way to enact the change. That's it! If it requires the government to raise taxes on the wealthy, tax businesses that consistently have windfall profits or cut military spending, then so be it. No excuses, no special interest manipulations, no more! Just say no. The American people are the decision makers as are stock holders in public companies. Lawmakers are hired to find the most cost effective way to implement change. The drafters of The Articles of Freedom and Democracy encouraged all Americans to mandate changes benefiting the majority of our citizens while relying on government to implement the laws in a fiscally responsible manner.

Whenever I read a sentence that starts with the words: Hey Stupid.... I immediately turn off. I do continue reading the passage though since it may be something funny or interesting. I hope you will do the same:

HEY STUPID! IT'S NOT THE PRESIDENT, IT'S MEMBERS OF CONGRESS!

Even the Tea Party financial backers try and remain anonymous by setting up shell organizations with patriotic names because they do not want any direct ties to these extremist groups in the event Tea Party recruits are unable to meet their prime objective of deceiving the public with unsubstantiated lies in support of their candidates. The extremists portray socialized government as the evil when it is really large corporations and now wealthy individuals who are subsidizing fringe groups to spin the real truth only to further their own self-interests. Why would we want to overthrow our current government while eliminating social programs designed to protect all Americans? The Tea Party patriots are being trained in aggressive tactics to take control of this country from the current rule of government should things not go as they planned with their choice of lawmakers. Sound familiar with what is going on not only in other countries today but starting to happen in this country as well, albeit on a smaller scale so far. Remember the Cliven Bundy fiasco that happened earlier this year in Nevada? The Bureau of Land Management was just trying to collect the grazing fees past due from this rancher for his use of government land to raise his livestock. Other ranchers in the area have similar agreements with the BLM and understand the language of the contract each signed when entering into the agreement with this government agency. Bundy's troubles with the government started almost twenty years ago when he refused back then to renew his cattle grazing permit with BLM. Since he made no more effort to pay the required permit fees after that first encounter, a judge in 1998 told him he must vacate the land he had leased for grazing his cattle on because he was in violation of his agreement with BLM. Fast forwarding to present day events. This particular conservative taker in our society, pouted and stamped his feet while making outrageous claims on Fox News about all the injustices within our current form of government, as local sheriffs tried to remove him from the property for trespassing. How dare the US Government force him to pay on the lease agreement he signed over twenty years ago and was currently in arrears for over a million dollars! You probably know the rest of the story but let me just highlight what happened after that since it is a statement where this country is heading unless we get gun control in check. Of course immediately after this emotional cry for reinforcements from Bundy on Fox News, the Tea Party militia shows up to defend this deadbeat from justice being carried out by the authorities just trying to do their jobs. It was so shocking to see the Tea Party militia on the highway overpass above the property in question, aiming their military grade automatic weapons squarely at the government officials and local authorities, daring any of them from making the first move! Fox News commentators were feeding fuel to the fire by condemning our government on the air while praising this national hero, in their eyes, and his brave supporters. It was one more example how angry and dangerous conservatives have become when their beliefs are challenged by others. Scary, I think.

Let's keep voting this radical faction of individuals into public office under the guise of smaller government so a congregation of 'red neck white guys gone wild,' can finally put an end the chaos in Washington and lift the oppression so many citizens are feeling today by returning the colonies back to some semblance of order that we had over two hundred years ago. The spin doctor's will stop at nothing to convince us that government is evil when in fact it is the only entity powerful enough and financially solvent enough to save us from our own bad decisions or unfortunate situation we may find ourselves in someday. Who is going to provide you and your family the safety net of health care and the funds to survive once you reach a certain age or become disabled? What if you were unable to save for a time in your life when you or a family member were out of work and needed assistance financially or had medical needs and could not pay for them? Well some politicians and radical Tea Party members are working to try and take that safety net away from you and your family because they truly feel those unfortunate citizens receiving aid from the government are drains on society and would be better off just vanishing off the face of the earth or dealing with their negative situations on their own. It is ironic since many of the foot solders supporting the directive of the Tea Party patriots, and present at the majority of their rallies, are for the most part themselves on the government dole in some form or another. Republicans, conservatives and obstructionists fought to prevent those on unemployment from receiving the safety net because in their own words, "it prevented them from looking for another job." That safety net plus Social Security and Medicare were funded by the hard working people of this country and the intent of those trusts being setup by our government was to assure the funds would be available in a time of need, for all working class citizens. The monies collected for those programs was placed in trusts for a reason, to be there when people who paid into them while in the workplace, needed it later in their lives. It was never designed for lawmakers to use the funds for their own pet projects. These same compassionate spin doctor's want to privatize Social Security and Medicare for seniors and disabled citizens because they have made so many bad investments with our money in the past and the funds are now so greatly depleted, they are starting to realize that investing the small amount left in the trusts should be done by the professionals on Wall Street, for a slight fee. Being self employed for over 25 years I contributed the employer and employee portion of withholding towards my retirement. I am a pacifist by nature but let it be known to all, no one better try and take my entitlement away from me and sell it to the highest bidder on Wall Street or I may find myself enlisting in that Tea Party militia to try and stop them! Just so you know, I have a 22cal. rifle somewhere with a beautiful solid walnut stock and a clip that holds at least 7 bullets from what I remember. Don't anyone mess with my Social Security savings or else! Oh yeah and I live on a hill with a keen vantage point of the surrounding area. Bring it on sonny!

The message is clear by some in Washington, those currently taking advantage of the entitlements owed to them are reducing the chances for these funds to be available later for the wealthy and their families should they ever need them. After all, those without wealth and power are inferior and expendable beings in the eyes of the elite.

It is past time to put a stop to the greed and abuse of power, remove the abusers and return control of this fine country back to its citizens. I am still perplexed when I read about a political figure doing something that appears on the face as a genuine and compassionate concern for the struggles facing minority populations in this country today. Like Senator Rand Paul of Kentucky planning a trip to Guatemala during his upcoming summer break to show his concern for the plight of the migrant children coming into this country illegally or not. In addition, he claims he will be providing free eye exams to a select few while there since he needs to stay current on his ophthalmology training in the event his current career in Congress ever ends. Immediately after the Senators' announcement, the front man for the GOP Latino community started playing up this humanitarian gesture by the senator as further proof that he would make a good president in 2016 because of his unwavering support for the Latino's in this country coming in 'legally.' Of course Rand Paul still believes that private business owners should be able to segregate the patrons of their businesses by race and color of their skin, but hey, we shouldn't discount the value of free eye exams! You really need to look a little deeper folks! Hey, I was born an almost poor white child in the South so I can say folks, folks. Take a few minutes and look into the true character of someone before showing support for them just because occasionally they demonstrate some small and superficial display of caring.

It is time to put a stop to the status quo system, support a new system of Manifest Destiny and regain our unalienable rights as free citizens in a democratic society once again.

I challenge anyone in Washington to face me and the American people and openly express your willingness to work with us and genuinely want to help improve *our* quality of life on this earth, and fulfill *our* needs and desires first and foremost above your own. Senator Bernie Sanders from Vermont is one of those tireless crusaders fighting for the rights of all the people and who should be a role model for other lawmakers to look up to as their mentor. I know some members of Congress don't like their official title of "Public Servant", but that is your job title and job description all in one, so either accept that and perform the duties you swore to uphold upon entering office, or step aside so Senator Sanders can get something done for the people of this country. As stated before, America has grown tired of your antics! If you were employed in the private sector and performed under your own agenda, took bribes in return for favors and essentially told your boss where to stick it, you would be fired for insubordination and investigated for unlawful actions, and that is exactly what I am going to propose later in the book as a way of dealing with the current toxic atmosphere in Washington.

It is time for the obstructionist, the do nothing party and those motivated by greed and self fulfilling ideals, to step aside and let the rest of us reshape the way our government was intended to be run, by the people and for the people.

The Justice Dept, the IRS, the Veterans Administration are just a few of the agencies in need some radical overhauls so that our current form of government can operate more efficiently and effectively once again. Congress has raided the budgets of these agencies to a point that they are unable to run effectively without the needed oversight. The outcome, with all of the 'Scandals' being investigated today in committee, could have been prevented if Congress had not cut the funding from these agencies to a point where they could not operate effectively due solely to the lack oversight. I guess that shortfall in the budgets has not been an issue to bring up in all the 'scandals' being investigated today in committee. Congress is a classic example of a branch of government gone rogue due to its members being allowed to work in an environment without direct supervision. The current administration is trying tirelessly to right the sinking ship inherited from the previous administration, albeit with complete resistance from the conservatives who feel the status quo is still our only salvation. Been there done that, unsuccessfully.

So let's move on! It's like one of our great comedians so eloquently stated in "Show me the Buffet." No one should be allowed to graze at a buffet because the line is long and people are hungry waiting in line. Pick up the food, put it on your tray and move on but don't hold up the line debating if you want two kinds of vegetables or not! There are so many non-issues pending before Congress today that lending further debate to these matters has become pointless for most Americans including the lawmakers who wrote the bills. The House in Congress won't even allow anything substantive to come to the floor for a vote because they know passage would be swift and with little fanfare. What's the fun of not messing with other peoples lives when you are in control and blocking the line at the buffet! Besides, lawmakers still get their exorbitant paychecks week after week while remaining accountable to no one for their anemic job performances, so why change.

Every living being on this planet should be able practice their own personal beliefs as long as those ideals and beliefs are personal and are not imposed on someone else. The political system in this country and members of Congress in particular operate contrary to this and instead try and manipulate the populous into believing that in their positions as political leaders that they are the only authorities on those matters affecting each and everyone of us personally.

Getting on with our lives in a progressive, forward direction has now become a time-sensitive matter to be addressed with the utmost urgency by all those given the power to enact those changes, sometimes referred to as members of Congress. We no longer have the luxury of time to debate non-issues in this country. Use the impending destruction of this planet through global warming to find other ways to meet our energy needs or explore other galaxies for planets to inhabit once earth is too hazardous to exist on. Let educators debate the causes and extremity that climate change will have on us as a civilization while lawmakers create jobs in space exploration and developing alternative energy sources. I would really like to see in my lifetime, aside from the exploration other planets, that politics and governing in this country be separated, though I know that the odds of either happening for some time are pretty remote.

Chapter 1

The Problem

America is in a holding pattern. There is stormy weather in every direction. The turbulence makes it impossible to land and there isn't enough fuel to get above the weather. Any suggestions? I know, let's sue the president to distract the public from the critical issues facing all Americans today and the fact that lawmakers are MIA. In their defense, lawmakers have not been able to find an equitable balance between work and scheduled vacation time to commit to anything substantive with their workload, so lighten up people.

We have a climate of uncertainty and a greater disregard for our fellow man and woman than ever before. In this state of weakness and vulnerability good citizens are being manipulated into believing the root of the problem is in our government. Most people are angry, insecure and acting without compassion for the strife of so many Americans today. The conservative, right wing faction is working 24/7 to agitate and divide the citizens of this great country. They have no solutions to any of the problems we face as a society except to find fault with everyone who expresses views different than theirs. Unfortunately they just have views and ideas that have no substance and no tangible meaning to anyone but themselves. As they throw out the following words: jobs, lower taxes, smaller government, huge deficit, black president, privatize entitlements, send migrant children home in steerage, lower wages, women's place is in the home, my gun has more rounds than your gun has, slavery had its benefits for some, and on and on and on, in the end they are just words. What does this all mean? I see most dialogue today as purposeless, meaningless words that conger up images of something good through association for a few, period. The words: 'lower taxes' just like 'good sex' are mere words that make people look outside their uneventful lives even if only for a few seconds. It does nothing to address finding a solution to the problems facing the current and future generations in the country. Well maybe 'good sex' won't hurt to shift our focus for the moment away from the real problems at hand. Conservatives and obstructionists point their finger at the president as if he is the problem, but all it does is provide a smoke screen away from the real issues at hand. Do lawmakers really think throwing out talking points on their way to the airport while leaving Washington for yet more time off, makes for a convincing argument to the American people that they have things under control? I'm not feeling the warmth yet, but maybe someday soon. Many living in rural America have been able to function just fine in their day to day lives simply by hearing the sound bites espoused according to the gospel of Rush, but mainstream America has too many real and pressing obstacles placed in front of them every day of their lives to be able exist that way.

Speaking of rural America, I did the pioneering, homesteading thing for about twenty-five years myself but have to admit, my priorities, due to my age at the time and strange environment I found myself living in, were different back then. We had our own rule of law and belief system in 'back of beyond' but having to drive down the mountain everyday to run a high-tech company in Silicon Valley forced me to adapt to the more universal rules of law that governed society as a whole. The only time we paid any attention to Washington back then was when lawmakers tried to infringe on our space and inflict their demands on us that were contrary to everything we were taught about right and wrong when growing up. My generation questioned everything these so called authorities told us were mainstream beliefs and that we as a subculture known as hippies, needed to get onboard with this way of thinking. Things like when the alert was posted that the communist are coming, the communist are coming! What, I wouldn't know a communist sympathizer if I passed one on the street or saw one at Starbucks drinking a large latte! European history was not my strong point in school so the only communists I ever remember reading about were in the USSR. So when our government told us that the communists are coming and not the Russians are coming, I knew something smelled oh so foul, and knew then it did not originate in Denmark! With the conflict originating in Vietnam, and the only thing I knew about Asia at the time was how much I liked Sweet and Sour Pork, I personally had no issues with the people of this county. So when America declared war on Vietnam and asked for volunteers to go to this strange land and eradicate those practicing this evil belief system before they came to our shores to try and indoctrinate our people to believe as they did, the young men in my generation started to question what was really going on here.

We really thought we had this simpatico relationship with our government at the time and just wanted to make love not war! It became quickly apparent that others were not buying this 'shuck & jive' that our political leaders were trying to sell to the public because low and behold, the draft system magically appeared before our eyes. This lead me to believe that even with the sign-up bonuses offered to clueless volunteers stepping up to save our country from the onslaught of those evil-doers, that wasn't incentive enough to fill the bus before heading overseas. Fortunately for me and most of my friends we had student deferments and high lottery numbers that prevented us from going to fight yet another needless war and killing thousands of innocent people for reasons not really known to anyone outside of Washington. Even with all the protections given to middle class white young people against being drafted, some of our numbers were rapidly approaching being called. I just remember sitting around with my friends on several occasions and trying to weigh worst case scenarios to consider if we were actually called to duty. None of us were very macho types except in our own minds, so the thought of actually shooting at someone or worse yet being shot at, led us to think about the only other option we had, Canada! Yikes, not that, although none of us knew anything about that place north of us, we just knew it was not on our top ten list of places to visit in our lifetime, especially when not knowing how long a layover it may turn out to be. We did all agree how much we liked their bacon though. Anyway, none of us had any success learning foreign languages in school much less the English language. I remember we would have long debates around the keg wondering exactly where the 'Aye' was supposed to be in the sentence when speaking Canadian.

That was when my generation of young men really began questioning authority and not acting on anything the bureaucrats would say as gospel until we researched further that perhaps they may have some underlying agenda behind this attempt to change our core beliefs. The point is everyone should question what someone else says unless we have a personal relationship with the person and know their intentions are honorable. Just as our past fearless leader spoke, "fool me once, shame on…fool me twice and… shame on…. don't do that again."

Some people certainly do not want to hear this but as I see it, the root of all that is wrong with America today evolves around responsibility, or better yet people not accepting any responsibility for their own actions. Yikes, that hurt man! "It's not my fault" is the modern day response to everything gone bad in someone's life. If you want to see just how epidemic the problem has become in America today just watch a few episodes of Judge Judy to see how out of touch people have become with their role in society by accepting no responsibility for their actions towards another person. Just when I thought someone's performance on the show was Oscar material, another person will come on the show and take the new leadership position in the blame game.

I don't fault the young people today for not being able to differentiate between levels of responsibility they need to take for their acts, but no one has blanket immunity from their actions simply by believing that it has to be some one else's fault for the situation they currently find themselves in. When our role models today teach us to just blame someone else for the problems that we as individuals find ourselves in, and not even argue any rational defense for the situation at the moment, then what do you expect people to do. "S___ happens" sounds like an acceptable defense to me!

Lawmakers have paved the pathway to easy street for people today by providing an excuse for a once responsible society to just pass the blame on to others for the problems we all face individually. For instance, lawmakers are quick to blame the president for not turning the economy around quicker than he has. That sounds good to me, what's for lunch! Lawmaker's distract us from the truth by blaming someone else for the slow turnaround in the economy only to continue contributing to the problem as they offer no solutions to correct any of the injustices facing most Americans today. People should only be given so many free passes in life before they have to admit they are wrong and take responsibility for their actions before someone else is harmed as a result of their cavalier and destructive attitude. In a conscience abuse of power by those in a position of authority and by setting this current day precedence that it is acceptable practice for *all* citizens to no longer accept responsibility for their own actions, then the tragic shooting at Sandy Hook Elementary School is a precursor for more needless acts to follow. Those individuals who commit such egregious acts against all humanity certainly do not accept any responsibility for their crimes while concluding that it must be someone else's fault for who they have become today.

There is far more enrichment in life to be part of the solution than part of the problem. You can continue to side with the Tea Party conservatives and continue to point the finger at all the injustices you perceive in life, or you can begin to find purpose with your existence on this planet and reach out to those who truly want to be part of the solution with those crucial issues facing all Americans today.

I often wonder how people can claim to be loving and responsible parents if they are ignoring the direction this country is heading and essentially ignoring the fact that their children and their children's children are facing a world with no future as long as we do nothing to change the current course we are on. Climate change may seem like a conspiracy theory now and only an occasional, if any, inconvenience to you and your loved ones. If you think of yourself as a responsible and caring parent though and there is even the slightest chance you are placing your children or grandchildren at risk by ignoring possible cataclysmic change in our weather patterns, then I just hope you won't be around to try and apologize when your family faces the pain and suffering that follows an extreme climate event.

I need to pose this question again because I think it needs to be on all our minds as we navigate the challenges of life before each of us. If you put all your past and present ideals, beliefs and prejudices aside and just ask this one question I am sure most people in this country will come up with the same response: What have the majority of our elected officials ever done for us or our families to directly improve the quality of life we've experienced during our short time on this planet? The answer will be almost unanimous: little to nothing! Unless you are wealthy or politically connected, you and I only represent to those in power, a means to attain their self-serving goals in life, which is to become more prosperous and powerful on the backs of every hard working American.

Some catastrophic event may be required in this country for people to put their differences aside and ban together to provide comfort to those most in need. Having experienced and lived through three downturns in our economy and one natural disaster, I have witnessed the capacity in people to demonstrate compassion for each other in a time of need. The uncertain times we as a society find ourselves in today are being overshadowed and almost diminished by those responsible for its mere existence. The evil doers are deflecting the truth about their involvement in the current crises by finding fault with those trying to right their misdeeds. They have absolutely no solutions to offer other than to do nothing. The message is even more absurd than that, they are saying put them back in charge so they can guarantee the status quo and assure the only change they will support is tax cuts for the wealthy and declaring war on other countries we have no business challenging their personal beliefs in the first place. And even more extreme than all this empty rhetoric is that because people are so angry and disillusioned with the current establishment they feel their only option now is to side with the fringe extremists promising changes that are so way out that it almost seems comical. These people add laughter to our mundane lives, only thing is that we are laughing at them instead of with them as they choose to live their lives in their own reality while ignoring the pain and suffering they are causing to so many during their quest for fame and power. If people truly believe that the ideals superficially espoused by the Tea Party establishment will make our lives better on this planet, may God have mercy on all our souls because life as we currently know it will change for ever. And I don't mean that in a good way. It may be time to revisit those Second Amendment remedies so eloquently espoused by Sharron Angle while running for Republican Senator of Nevada in 2010. I may even need to put my glasses on to find that bullet clip for my rifle if things continue to escalate as they have been towards the dark side.

The previous administration encouraged predatory lending, risky investment products and adversity to regulation of financial institutions. Bush II used to boast that during his administration more people than any time in the history of the country were living the American dream through owning their own homes. Though when the smoke screen disappeared and reality set in it became apparent that the illusion once again benefited only those in power. The financial institutions amassed windfall profits while causing unimaginable suffering to millions of hard working Americans who lost everything to a well orchestrated scam. In addition the Bush administration and its reckless spending for needless wars and tax breaks for the wealthy, eventually caused the worst economy and job losses since the Great Depression. In their own words: "Mission Accomplished."

When are the American people going to finally realize that many of their elected officials are in their position to fulfill self-interests over what's in the best interests of their constituents. Voters quickly forget that politicians consistently make promises they rarely keep, even if they have the best intentions of doing so before going into office. With each election voters want to believe that change will finally happen to benefit them if their choice of politicians are elected into office. The real problem is that the system currently in place simply will not allow the populous to decide on issues that affect them the most. Only their elected representatives can speak on their behalf, and as we have seen, they rapidly forget who gave them their jobs to start with and who will bid the highest for their loyalty. And to add insult to injury, sometimes even the popular vote for president is overruled by those bratty kids over at Electoral College, as we saw in the Bush II second term victory. Who are these kids anyway?

What if the system allowed the taxpayers to vote on every issue that needed changing with the exception of matters of national security or those needing an immediate remedy by the president and his administration.

This is the only way that I see the will of most Americans finally being realized and change brought about quickly and effectively. The real meaning of a democratic society ruled by the people and for the people would once again ring true to the desires of our forefathers in writing the Declaration of Independence.

Did you know that America's first President, George Washington, did not belong to a political party. Most of America's founding fathers were opposed to political parties, and wanted none of them in the United States of America.

The two party system in America evolved to prevent one party from gaining too much power, by creating a second party with opposite policies. **There is currently no provision, nor has there ever been one in our Constitution, mandating a two party system.**

The current party system in America is exactly what the founding fathers abhorred about allowing such a process to be enacted. It breeds self-serving, ego driven motives surrounding one purpose – greed. Our representatives do not advocate for the beliefs of the citizens who elected them but rather for the special interests bidding the highest for their needs first and foremost.

Do you think our founding fathers would have endorsed the practice of special interests buying support from lawmakers to further their agenda over the needs of our citizens? That a suit with a checkbook could walk outside their office and down the street to "purchase" a favor from someone who was entrusted to represent the people's needs first and foremost. How did our government become so corrupt? The answer is simple– abuse of power and greed by those elected into office through false pretenses and with the public allowing them to get away with it.

I would like to believe that it all started innocently, where no one was really supposed to get hurt. Where someone or some group had an agenda or set of values they needed to gain support with. Having the power to "convince" another person to believe in your ideals, constitutes a form of brainwashing. If it is a moral or spiritual belief perhaps it is harmless. If it is a political agenda benefiting a few, it can be the most destructive form of manipulation. Such as the case made by our government leaders justifying most wars we have entered into.

The time has come and we the people have a process put in place by our founding fathers to demand change if our "Form of Government becomes destructive of these ends".

We hold these truths to be self-evident, that all men are created equal, that they are endowed by their Creator with certain unalienable Rights, that among these are Life, Liberty and the pursuit of Happiness.-- That to secure these rights, Governments are instituted among Men, deriving their just powers from the consent of the governed, --**That whenever any Form of Government becomes destructive of these ends, it is the Right of the People to alter or to abolish it, and to institute new Government, laying its foundation on such principles and organizing its powers in such form, as to them shall seem most likely to effect their Safety and Happiness.**

For too many years our elected officials have spent recklessly, made self-serving decisions not in our best interest and the most heinous act of all, wasted our precious time on this earth suppressing our ability to pursue the 'American Dream' in health, wealth and happiness while being able to practice goodwill towards our fellow man.

The Obama administration has spent the previous 6 years since taking office trying to correct the pre-meditated, negative impact the past administration had on this country. The politicians, always knowing what is right for the American people have been like children fighting to get their own way instead of coming together to work with the president to make positive changes. Barack Obama has not always made the right decisions to try and get America back on its feet, but at least he is not ignoring the situation while presenting solutions that may have a positive impact on the people. Hey, he has two young children who will inherit any residual from the previous administration that he was not able to change during his 2nd and final term in office. Even then, he still puts the needs of the country first over those of himself and his family, to assure other young people will have opportunities and fulfill their dreams someday. Proof of that is seen during every public appearance he makes when placing the needs of regular people, as he addresses them by their individual names, above what the government wants in return. Unlike lawmakers who rarely, if ever, address the hardships so many American's are facing today while speaking to them on the same level as the president does consistently!

It's not only time to eliminate the predominant two party system in this country today, but once the new government is in place, hold all those accountable for their pre-meditated, self serving acts against humanity.

When in the Course of human events, it becomes necessary for one people to dissolve the political bands which have connected them with another, and to assume among the powers of the earth, the separate and equal station to which the Laws of Nature and of Nature's God entitle them, a decent respect to the opinions of mankind requires that they should declare the causes which impel them to the separation.

Let me not get ahead of myself though and concentrate on the limited control remaining for voters to try and change the negative state of affairs we now find ourselves in today. Everyone of voting age should get out in the next election and vote your conscience and principals. This is such an important election please don't feel that your vote will not count or don't just settle for the candidate promising to make a difference this time around once in office. Seriously, search your souls and reinforce the decision that completing what has already been accomplished so far by the current administration may not be all that bad, as some are making it sound like. If things don't always work as you expect in life, then you need to get over it and move on to fight another day. Life, as we all have learned to accept, is full of disappointments, but just remember that you are the sole owner of the situation you find yourself in today and if you are unhappy where you are then know this, you are the only one who can change that for yourself. If you are lacking in the self-confidence and strength to fight for what you believe, then continue to wallow in self-pity and blame someone else for all that is wrong with your life today. Many lawmakers running for re-election and those currently seeking office for the first time continue to prey on the weaknesses of people like yourself by promising that once again they have your backs and will help you get through your rough patches just like they always have in the past. Not!

The people can truly feel vindicated after the next election by letting the wealthy funders spend all the money they want to try and win friends and influence voters during this next cycle. You know that you can always hit the mute button on your remote or pre-record your favorite TV shows and fast forward through the commercials while ignoring their propaganda campaigns of lies and deceit endorsing the candidates of their choosing, not yours. Then go to the poles on election day and show the pundits once and for all that the people want their country back and prepared to do so! Sorry Sheldon, but the house lost their bet one more time! Place your bets for the odds of your candidate winning in the next election. I would start to rethink who you are placing your bets on though because with 'Mr. 47%' and the 'Newtster,' you are currently 2 for 2 with your ill advised predictions of the past.

I am so glad I decided early in life to take control of my own destiny and follow my intuitions for what was the right and wrong path to go down on my journey to fulfillment. I gained as much strength and forward direction from my mistakes as I did from my successes throughout life. I would have never been where I am today with such a strong base of knowledge if I had not at least tried different things in life. Talk is, and will ever be, just words unless followed by some form of substantive and tangible action.

Chapter 2

Freedom Of Speech

The 1st amendment of the US Constitution defines the intent of the law as drafted by our forefathers:

Freedom of speech is the freedom to speak without *censorship* and/or *limitation*. The synonymous term **freedom of expression** is sometimes used to indicate not only freedom of verbal speech but any act of seeking, receiving and imparting information or ideas, regardless of the medium used. In practice, the right to freedom of speech is not absolute in any country and the right is commonly subject to limitations, such as on "*hate speech*".

The right to freedom of speech is recognized as a *human right* under Article 19 of the *Universal Declaration of Human Rights* and recognized in *international human rights law* in the *International Covenant on Civil and Political Rights* (ICCPR). The ICCPR recognizes the right to freedom of speech as "the right to hold opinions without interference. Everyone shall have the right to freedom of expression". *[1][2]* Furthermore freedom of speech is recognized in European, inter-American and African regional human rights law. It is different from and not to be confused with the concept of *freedom of thought*. The freedom of speech can be found in early human rights documents, such as *Declaration of the Rights of Man and of the Citizen* (1789), a key document of the *French Revolution.[4]* The Declaration provides for freedom of expression in Article 11, which states that: "The free communication of ideas and opinions is one of the most precious of the rights of man. Every citizen may, accordingly, speak, write, and print with freedom, but shall be responsible for such abuses of this freedom as shall be defined by law."*[5]*

Every citizen may accordingly speak, write and print with freedom, **but shall be equally responsible for such abuses of this freedom as shall be defined by law.** When was this interpreted to mean every citizen has the right to speak freely even if someone else is harmed as a result of your slanderous contempt against another persons character? The majority of Americans are becoming defensive and distrustful of their civic leaders as they lose all trust in their ability to represent them honestly and with any sense of integrity. They see these 'leaders' whom they trusted with their lives and livelihood, essentially ignore the people who gave them their jobs in the first place. These racist, homophobic, religious fanatics are preaching to a small congregation of followers though. President Obama seems well aware of how counter productive and ineffective it is to blame someone else for the problems he inherited when trying to concentrate on finding solutions to remedy the situations at hand. The time it takes to defend your actions could be used to remedy the problem. Citizens are becoming disenchanted with the finger pointing by members of Congress while the president has been reluctant to defend all the positive changes made so far under his administration. Fortunately, better late than never, we are finally starting to see, with two years and a few months left to go for this president, that he is finally defending his actions by calling out the Republicans in Congress for their obstructionist tactics. They have loosely interpreted the First Amendment as they have with other amendments to the Constitution in an effort only to validate their campaigns of outright lies while maligning the president and deceiving the American people.

If this level of disparagement occurred in the private sector, those responsible for the misdeeds would be held accountable in a court of law. It should not be acceptable to disparage someone in public office and not face the same consequences as the law permits when the same egregious act is committed in the private sector. If the act is intentional and without merit or facts to support the narrative then those committing the malicious deed should be criminally charged in a civil court and have to pay monetary restitution to the harmed party. Just as in the private sector if someone's livelihood is diminished due to a deliberate and malicious character assassination, the perpetrator(s) can be sued in a court of law. There is currently no civil punishment for verbalizing, publishing or inciting others to defame a public figure with deliberate and malicious intent to cause harm to that person. Especially if you speak out against our president and tarnish his image in front of the people of this great nation, when there are no facts to support the allegations or justification to do so. And when it is done with malice of forethought for personal gain the act should be one of tyranny and punishable by a prison sentence, Lindsey Graham, Senator from South Carolina. Do you really think anyone else gets your derogatory remarks in public about President Obama or think they are cute or the least bit funny? Well do you punk? Only when there are severe consequences for those malicious attacks against another persons character in the public sector as in the private sector, will the evil doers think twice about committing such an act ever again. Doesn't anyone else see the fundamental injustice by some, with their continued abuse of this and other laws? If you want to change the First Amendment so that the law allows this egregious practice then so be it, but the more this injustice continues to proliferate in our society with no consequences for such deliberate acts, then it will soon become the accepted practice and just further the 'blame game' to a point of absurdity. I just hope we can clone Judge Judy because I fear the backlog of cases is about to become too overwhelming for one judge to handle! It also sets the stage for a society being transformed into one without the intellect to be able to differentiate between a lie and the truth. Sounds good, now what's for dinner? Repeat after me, it is just one word you need to say over and over and over and over again - *question everything*! Ok 2 words.

Any public figure on record stating their views and then later deceiving the public with a contradictory statement should be held to their original statement on record. The Republicans and conservative politicians currently in office who fought against the enactment of the stimulus package which was solely designed to help American citizens during the worst economy since the Great Depression, can't turnaround later and then take credit for the relief it provided to their constituents by misrepresenting to the public that they contributed to the solution instead of the problem.

Leo W. Gerard

President of the United Steelworkers International
Posted: December 22, 2008 04:36 PM

A week earlier, 31 GOP Senators, mostly from Southern states, voted to avert their eyes and allow American auto companies to die. They opposed $14 billion in federal loans for GM and Chrysler, revealing that their loyalty lies not with America, not even with their own states, but with South Korea and Germany and Japan.

They are Toyota Republicans.

Toyota has non-union manufacturing plants in Alabama, Kentucky, Mississippi and Texas - states whose senators led the GOP quest to slay the Big Three American auto manufacturers - Richard Shelby, R-Ala.; Mitch McConnell, R-Ky, and John Cornyn, R-Tx. Here's the Republican from Mississippi, Sen. Thad Cochran, explaining why he'd vote against the loans, "Things have changed. It's not just the Big Three anymore," he said, pointing out that Nissan and Toyota employ more Mississippians than General Motors, Ford and Chrysler. But, he said, the foreign companies would not share "in the benefits of that automobile bailout program."

No. But Mississippi did give Nissan and Toyota more than $650 million to entice them to locate in the state. GM, Ford and Chrysler didn't share in those benefits, Sen. Cochran. The Toyota Republicans are all for helping the rich with tax breaks and shelters, and they're all for aiding foreign auto manufacturers with billions worth of tax forgiveness and government-paid infrastructure improvements.

One of these Toyota Republicans even had the nerve to go to a United Autoworkers rally to take credit for the bailout of the Big Three and congratulate the workers for sticking it out until the automakers got back on their feet after the subsidy from the government. Even after he voted to let the US automakers go out of business so the foreign automakers could compete more freely in America! I am not making this stuff up, it is all documented on Wiki or somewhere else, believe me or better yet, look it up for yourself.

Are the American people so out of touch with seeing how these individuals are not only manipulating the system but outright deceiving the citizens of this great country solely for their own self interests! Even in a recent primary runoff in Mississippi people in that state overlooked Sen. Cochran's track record and voted him the winner of the challenge against Chris McDaniel. Of course this was one of those elections where it was better to support the lesser of two evils in the runoff or consequences may have been even greater if McDaniel won. Although I know McDaniel is a sore loser and still not conceded in the race, do you really don't want him or even Cochran now, representing the people of your state in the future? Think of this as a wake up call to really show your true convictions in the next election and tell them all to take a hike by voting someone in to office who will start to look after the needs of the people in that state for a change. Expanding Medicaid to cover more of the uninsured in your state would be a great start, an idea that no Republican supports!

Chapter 3

The Solution

Barack Obama could be the greatest president, 'for the people' as he already is 'by the people', this country has ever seen, if he were just allowed to be. When a business, as was this country just 6 years ago, is on the brink of collapse, a visionary is brought in to try save it from potential collapse. Similar to what the president did to save the American auto companies during his first term in office. There is a deliberate and well calculated campaign in America to discredit the current administration and try to cause it, and the country behind, to fail. The threat on the right is real, their purpose is self-serving and subversively racist while the outcome of their agenda, if allowed to play out, would negatively impact every man, woman and child in this country in the near future and especially for future generations to try and live with the now irreversible change in their lives. This is our last chance to find some purpose within each of us and stand by the leader of the free country to help him make all our lives better while assuring we can live in peace and harmony among our fellow citizens.

President Obama is that visionary and seems compassionate in his ideals to turn this country around while trying to reverse the devastation to our nation that was intentionally orchestrated through the malfeasance of previous administration. The American people voted this president in for two terms for the same reason that the prophecies predict the Coming of The Messiah. The American people know we need someone of almost divine powers to save us from the direction this country was moving towards. Believe the polls if you wish, but I think that the majority of Americans are still holding out hope for this president to make good on the promises he made to all Americans in 2008 and again in 2012. Unfortunately he is not a God but simply a mortal human being trying to dig this country out of the deep hole started back in 2000, eight years prior to Barack Obama becoming president. It is human nature to make the wrong decisions at times, but the president, as we should all do, is taking personal responsibility for trying to correct what is primarily an inherited mess that he started tackling his first day in office. Remember the whole issue about taking responsibility for our actions, and how easy it is to identify where someone stands by their either being part of the problem or continuing to kick any solutions down the road for future generations to deal with.

In the private sector if you walked into a new job with the expectations of turning the department around from the chaos left by your predecessor and you were unable to do so, what do you think your boss would do during your next review? Would the employer react the same way if you showed some progress to turning things around while always demonstrating a sincere effort to do what was expected of you? If your associates stymied every attempt you made to turn things around and therefore contributing to your failures, then *they and they* alone would be responsible for the initial objective not being met under your watch. That would be one instance where it would be alright for you to point the finger at others and say failure this time wasn't your fault but theirs.

The New York Times – September 11, 2010 A GOP Leader Tightly Bound to Lobbyists by Eric Lipton -

"Mr. Boehner won some of his first national headlines in 1996 after he was caught handing out checks from tobacco lobbyists to fellow Republicans on the House floor. They intentionally ignored the obvious signs of industries operating without oversight so the principals of these businesses could continue to feed their incessant appetite of greed. I cannot think of one thing lawmakers, mostly conservative ones, have ever tried to do for the common citizen. Can you? So why do we keep electing politicians that make empty promises that they rarely, if ever, keep? Or even worse allowing these crooks to remain in office without being held accountable for their criminal actions! The message being sent to the most impressionable members of our society is: the only way to get ahead in life is through greed and deceit while demonstrating total contempt for mankind. Why aren't parents talking with their children about right and wrong and how the actions of some people causing crimes against humanity should be condemned not praised. I am certain most parents would rather take the easy way out though by insulating their children from the harsh realities of life during adolescence and let them find out on their own once they become adults. After all social morals and family values are a thing of the past with no place in modern day families. Hey that's good, could you text that message over to Joe to see!

The first thing the American people have to do is recognize that the founding fathers fought with their lives to ensure every man, woman and child had unalienable rights to live free, prosper and pursue happiness in a democratic society. These rights have now been taken away from the majority of law abiding American citizens. Politicians have sold the American people out to special interests. Greed drives those in power with no regard or compassion for human nature. So we need to get through the next few elections then concentrate to reorganize the institutions of government so that policy decisions affecting the lives and livelihood of the majority of citizens in this country are made by voters, not politicians. The people should be decision makers on living wages, job creation, universal health care and equal rights for everyone, while the government acts to find the most fiscally responsible way to enact laws, then administer the changes while providing the oversight required. We must never allow any of our federal agencies or branches of government to act independent of the laws that govern their own work ethics or our society as a whole. Congress's job is to come to a consensus on bills to be presented to other members for a vote then to find the most cost effective ways to implement and manage passed measures before being eventually signed into law. If they need to raise taxes on the wealthy or on corporations to pay for universal health care then make it so, and by the way, keep your opinions to yourselves as to whether you think the proposed law will work or not. I don't want to see any of those puppy dog tears 'tan man' because, take a deep breath, the people really don't care what you think personally about what is in 'our' best interest. Sorry man, I know the truth hurts, oh that's right 'truth' is not in your peoples' vocabulary.

I know your boss in the private sector could care less if you started moping around and making excuses because you didn't want to do a task assigned to you, regardless of whether it was in your job description or not. I am sure if lawmakers didn't like their jobs because they were not getting their way anymore, or couldn't inject their opinions into mainstream beliefs, the line would be out the door of Congress applying for their six figure income position once they quit!

In order to take back what is rightfully ours and start to run the government in a more streamlined fashion, I would like to propose the following ideas for all American's to think about once the ship is finally lifted off the sandbar:

- Define the will of the people as a minimum of 51% of all registered voters. With the exception of electing a president every four years I see no benefit with the public voting to bring other officials into office. Everyone with the exception of the president can go through a routine hiring process so that performance evaluations are maintained through Human Resources for employees of the government. If Amendments 17 and 20 of the Constitution need to be modified to show members of Congress being hired into their positions instead of elected by the people, then so be it. If members of Congress had not so abused their positions of power as we see today, then this would not even be an issue. The people know that the once honored and respected institution known as Congress has now become this adversarial institution in government that needs immediate attention if it is going to be redefined and turned back its original intent, as drafted in our US Constitution. During the four year cycle of electing a president, initiatives could be voted on at anytime by the public. If say universal healthcare is proposed and then passed by 51% of voters, then next it needs to go to Congress for its members to debate ways to best implement into law, with the most cost effective and timely process possible. If Congress delays the bill/initiative with going into effect for more than say 6 months, then they need to explain to the American people why. If they need additional time to increase budget levels or raise taxes to pay for the measure then keep the people posted on the progress being made. And never forget, as in the private sector if you cop an attitude and start stamping your feet because you have no say with the intent of the bill and want to keep your job, get over it! Because the American people could care less what your personal opinion is in the workplace. Either keep your thoughts, ideas, beliefs, convictions or old white guy ideals to yourself or bitch about how unjust life is in the break room with your fellow lawmakers. Remember though, your breaks are only 15 minutes each so talk amongst yourselves quickly so you can get your frustrations, that most Americans are now feeling, off your chest and then back to work.

- Develop the technology to allow each and every registered voter to make their voices be heard and counted electronically. At anytime and without prior notice, the government should send out a call for vote via phone, television or other device. Voters would have 24 hours to cast their vote on a measure that then goes to Congress for their pouting members to hash over and eventually signed into law by the president. As I said before, our time on this planet is too short to debate the pros and cons of everything that needs to be changed to improve our quality of life. The American people need to vote their beliefs while government agencies need to figure out the most cost effective and efficient manner in which to implement change, so that the measure to be voted on would be simple in description. For example: Your cell phone receives a call to vote. It is a text message stating the initiative: Would you like to have universal healthcare in this country where the government paid for all your medical needs in your lifetime allowing you and your family unlimited access to doctors and hospitals at no expense to you? If a citizen did not have a cell phone then maybe they could vote via email or land line phone once they supplied personal information confirming their identity. If the majority of the voters decided on a government subsidized healthcare system then it would become a mandate to be signed into law as soon as lawmakers developed a plan to best enact the measure. The reduction of costs for taxpayers to employ members of Congress under their new directive would be one way to help subsidize initiatives being signed into law. Lawmakers could probably perform the duties under their new job description with a starting salary of no more than $50,000 a year and they certainly won't need a travel budget or staff of their own! Measures or initiatives challenging our God given right for all citizens to choose what is best for them individually, would not even be recognized! Things like the right of every citizen to possess a military grade automatic weapon, would not even be considered to be brought to a vote. Equal rights for all! That could certainly be considered to be brought to a vote. No more restrictions on an individuals health and welfare choices. No more restrictions on religious beliefs. If you have a right to purchase a firearm to protect you or your family from potential harm, then keep it locked up in a safe place in your home, unless your profession requires you to carry a weapon in public. A private citizen carrying munitions into the public arena violates the right of another persons' freedom to object to that level of personal defense around others without equal protection, as I see it.

- With politicians and special interest lobbyists out of the way, the federal government should model itself after business entities whose mission it is to reward loyal employees with higher wages in return for their personal commitment to promote a more productive work environment. Government waste is so prevalent today that if agencies within the bureaucracy actually set up departments to run effectively and efficiently as seen in the private sector, the savings through redundancy of personnel and non-essential tasks could provide the additional funds needed for more comprehensive programs like entitlement based health care or larger cost of living increases for Social Security recipients. The people would still vote for a president to serve up to eight years unless he or she did not perform in their position to the satisfaction of the majority of voters. They could then be voted out after serving a minimum of 4 years and a new leader voted in during the next regular election cycle. The president would still have the power to appoint all federal positions as is currently done. The only difference will be since politics and party affiliation now has no role in government, Senate confirmation hearings for the candidates in consideration can still take place as directed under the Constitution but applicants could be interviewed based solely on their job qualifications, as is done in the private arena.

• Another thing we could vote on to stimulate the economy is expand the space program dramatically. Millions of jobs would be created through NASA and all the subcontractors needed to get us into outer space and explore other galaxies. The president has already expressed an interest in going to Mars in his lifetime. Not only are we rapidly running out of natural resources on this planet but we have no where else to go in the event we continue to ignore the signs climate change is impacting all our lives on a global level. Nonprofits like SETI Institute, through their continued alliance with private sector foundations and government agencies, could advocate for greater development of technologies to enable space travel for everyone and exploration to become a reality even sooner. Creativity and innovation, which has all but been outsourced from this country, would once again be invigorated and brought back through the quest to explore other planets and galaxies outside our own. We would once again take the lead in innovation and market our technological advances globally while closing the trade gap. Jobs would become plentiful once again in this country, but even more than that, **good jobs** would abound. Beam me up Scotty, I'll be one step closer to heaven then! Gadgets are cool and the public is always looking for a better cell phone with more features, but wouldn't it be nice to use some of our innovative expertise to develop ways off this planet in the event we all find ourselves walking on the scorched earth just to get to the market someday.

- We need to have a 4 day, 32 hour work week with everyone being paid a living wage to start. One day off during the month we could volunteer to help those less fortunate members of society feel that they still have meaning and purpose to their lives. On another day off during the month people should be required to attend a free concert paid for by the government. Name groups will have concerts all over the country every Friday in the month for all citizens to attend. **Music remains the only vehicle left that truly makes us drop our inhibitions and bring people together in peace and harmony.** Let's call it a mental health day. Wouldn't it be nice when your friends ask if you are going to the Bruce Springsteen concert or Mumford and Sons down at the park in town and your response is: 'it's the law, I'll be there!' Did you ever notice, with the exception of Altamont Speedway Festival in 1969, that people are free spirits, happy and smiling at each other while attending a concert and listening to their favorite music. Maybe those positive attitudes would eventually be carried over into the public arena more and more as we started to come together as one nation again. The remaining two days of the month should be spent doing something that engages families to spend more time together and start to rebuild that bond that connected us all together in the beginning. If you have no family nearby then take the dog for a walk or play with the cat. Dogs and cats, like corporations, are people too. Even if you use the time to reflect within or understand the importance of teaching future generations to develop greater family values, you will start to find purpose with your life on this planet. Those members of society, who already have the financial reserves beyond most peoples comprehension, need to willingly give back to your fellow citizens and allow them to enjoy some quality of life and realize the American dream as you yourselves have already been able to do. The very wealthy need to redistribute some of their wealth while mitigating the unsustainable income inequality so prevalent in today's society. Go to the recent report released by Standard & Poor's titled "How Increasing Inequality is Dampening U.S. Economic Growth, and Possible Ways to Change the Tide," for further guidance if needed.

- Unless a president can convince the American people that planned military conflicts outside our country are essential to enter into for our own safety here at home, then we need to think about redirecting those funds to protect our own borders instead. Maybe we could beef up the satellite defense system in this country in the event other countries pose a threat with attacking us on our soil, North Korea. We do need to rotate staff in those bunkers though so they don't become tired of waiting to push the button while falling asleep and accidently laying their heads down on the button. Those 'domes' as seen in the movies seem like a good idea also. The money we save by not having our military personnel deployed to other countries that we have no business being in without some support from our allies, could instead be used to strengthen and secure our borders here at home. If other countries want to contract out additional security details from one of our US based firms that specialize in that, then I'm sure there are a lot of mercenaries out their looking for extra work, instead of our country always supplying American troops and munitions to further their causes and ours too, I know.

- We have to stop giving money to other countries for the sole purpose of buying their allegiance. If it is for humanitarian reasons that Americans contribute taxpayer dollars to other governments, the case must be made that it will be used only for the intended cause and be a loan whenever possible. I was always suspicious when someone had to pay for friendship or buy allegiance from another party, when their association could be built on the premise of an equal partnership endeavor, such as the case with most humanitarian outreach goals.

- The single largest outlay of taxpayer dollars next to military spending is waste. Waste due to fraud, waste due to lack of oversight and waste due to lack of enforcement of the tax code and mismanagement of social programs designed to assist the disadvantaged population. The previous administration not only turned a blind eye to any oversight in banking and Wall Street but it encouraged creative instruments of investment to help its wealthy contributors get even wealthier at he expense of millions of hard working Americans losing their livelihoods. We could immediately put thousands of people to work on oversight committees. Workers could monitor Medicare claims that are batch processed to track fraudulent billing practices from health practitioners. How many tongue depressors does any one physician really need? Teams of workers could audit wealthy citizen's tax returns for fraudulent deductions or exemptions. These citizen oversight commissions could not only pay for themselves by identifying fraudulent claims made but also by providing backup information to the agencies cracking down on the repeat offenders through criminal investigations. Oversight commission staff would essentially be paid to 'rat out' those trying to cheat the government and maybe be given bonuses for bringing to justice, the primary offenders. Those sitting on citizen's oversight committees would make sure funds are being disbursed as intended through Medicare, Medicaid and Social Security. The current system of contracting out to private companies, to enforce the provisions regulating the claims process within our entitlement programs, is not working as well as it could. Without additional incentives offered to these private firms to crack down further on fraud and waste within our entitlement programs, abuses will continue within our current systems in place.

- We need to look at the way powerful lobbyists and legal professionals have manipulated the original intent of the language contained within the Amendments to the US Constitution. Let's start with the First Amendment and the liberties taken under the current interpretation of 'freedom of speech.' No one should be allowed to defame another individual without facing some consequences for such an offensive act. One of the most egregious acts committed against another individual is when The President of the United States is mocked or disrespected with no factual basis to support the speakers criticism. For example, when President Obama is represented as Hitler or the Joker or even a Marxist by the Tea Party radicals during a public assembly. Or when others create a commentary based on lies and disrespect towards another person with no regard to any truth or fact to support their statements. If the conservatives want to make false statements about President Obama then the president should be able to use public funds to hold them accountable in a court of law for slander and then have them prosecuted for a crime. The FCC should fine and eventually revoke the license of any news media outlet that continues to make false and defamatory statements against someone weather they are a political figure or not. The commentator making the false statements should be held personally liable for making accusations against another person with no proof or facts to back their unsubstantiated claims. The Second Amendment intent has been so skewed, solely to promote the agenda of the NRA by allowing them to advocate for the sale of more lethal weapons to private citizens. People really need to wake up and see what is going on before more innocent people in this country are murdered under the guise of self-preservation. I am sure the language in the law would have been crafted differently by the drafters of the Constitution if they had any forethought about the type of weapons that could be developed in the future. Things were different over two hundred years ago when dueling pistols and derringers were the only munitions available to private citizens. The weapons developed specifically for militia personnel at that time were prohibited for private citizens to obtain or own, unlike today. Most of the amendments to the Constitution need to be ratified or amended if they are to be transformed and aligned with today's laws of the land that all American's need to abide by. Any law containing ambiguity to its intent while being misinterpreted under current day 'rule of law' should require immediate revision to apply changes not foreseen by the drafters of the original document. The Second Amendment was very clear when written over two-hundred years ago: A well regulated Militia, being necessary to the security of a free State, the right of the people to keep and bear Arms, shall not be infringed. Even with my wildest and most vivid imagination sometimes I could never interpret that passage in the amendment to mean, that a private citizen has a right to keep and bear 'military grade automatic weapons'! Come on people just because certain lawmakers and the NRA believe what they are reading into the Second Amendment is true, it just isn't so! And if there is any doubt with the real intent of the amendments, when they were first drafted or last ratified, then amend them so all ambiguity is removed in order to provide absolute clarity with the intent in the 21st century. Question this stuff and demand change or I suggest that you and your family be fitted for bullet-proof vests as a precaution before going out in public again.

- The justice system is another area that needs to be changed. Special interests, specifically attorneys and judges have manipulated the intent of the laws to suit their own purpose. We are practically inviting criminals to commit crimes because they know through due process they will be given legal defense with certain rights to lessen or even overthrow their convictions. The only way we are going to deter criminals is hold them accountable for their crimes, especially those of sound mind and who cause intentional harm to another living being. If someone physically causes severe harm to another person more than once then they need to be incarcerated for the duration of their lives without any chance for parole. The people need to vote on changes to laws validated by the Supreme Court if their rulings bring into question some contradiction with the core personal beliefs of most citizens in this country. Corporations are people too, give me a break if anyone believes the basis behind that argument by a few public officials given too much power to begin with. Nine individuals should never be allowed to change laws such as the one they did with their ruling on Citizens United. It sets a new precedence in this country that money can buy power and that is very dangerous ruling if allowed to remain in existence. Justice Alito, shake your head all you want but the damage to this country is already done through your support with this ruling.

Someone committing a crime should never get a reduced sentence just for cooperating in their testimony against others involved in the same scheme. A criminal should never be released from custody due to a technicality with the way in which they were arrested. These are all interpretations and deliberate manipulations of the intent of the law for the sole purpose of sustaining the livelihood of attorneys and judges. Why do criminals who commit the most heinous crimes against other human beings deserve a public defender paid for by taxpayers? Why, because it creates jobs for attorneys and judges, many at taxpayer expense. The couple who kidnapped the young girl in California a while back, held her captive in a makeshift structure in their backyard for over 15 years. The man who abducted the young girl at the time forced her to conceive and then raise two children he was responsible for through his heinous acts. Call me vindictive, but I truly believe the couple that committed such a horrific act against another innocent living soul, a minor at the time, should both be sentenced to death for this heinous crime which they admitted to doing. Why do they even need a trial? Because attorneys and judges twist the intent of the law to give rights to criminals while providing themselves job security. It is as simple as that. Vote to send the attorneys and judges packing that defend the rights of criminals and put criminals where they deserve, behind bars or sent to another place where hopefully they can pay for their sins through eternity.

- Immigration reform has become such moral imperative and complicated issue to deal with, no one really wants to take an aggressive stance with solving the problem. Racial profiling as the State of Arizona has led the movement in is certainly not the answer when identifying whether someone has a right to be in this country or not. 'Papers Please' is such a abhorrent abuse of the law that the governor should have been recalled after her support of such a attack of everyone's civil liberties in this country. I know personally I will never step foot in that state again. Maybe we should start to address the problem by closing the borders completely, slowing the migrant influx into our country until we get more of our current citizens employed again and our economy turned around. Why compound the problem with greater competition for jobs, resources and social programs within our own country. The only way we are ever going to determine if someone really wants to work and provide for themselves and their family and not rely on subsidies is to provide opportunities to all citizens able and willing to work. The only way we can do that is to become a self-sufficient country again taking pride in 'Made in America.' If we can start to live within our means and be paid a living wage then we can start to work for less and bring manufacturing jobs back into this country. Many immigrants coming to America are hard working individuals willing to work for less and perform jobs others would rather not do. There is no reason we cannot grant citizenship to those members of our society willing to make a positive contribution and bring jobs back to America so we are not so dependent on foreign goods. Of course if opportunities are given but not taken because some able bodied citizens will never be motivated to make a positive contribution to society, then we should probably take away their safety net so they understand the need to be a part of the solution as opposed to always just contributing the problem.

- These are just some ideas that people should begin to think about once voting is made more accessible to each and every American citizen who is guaranteed that right in a democratic society such as ours. Citizens in this country should feel free be able to vote their own personal ideals and convictions while consciously conceding to the wishes of the majority will of the people. There are so many injustices in our current society just as there are so many positive attributes that give us hope and joy to be alive on this planet. I think most people would be truly content throughout their lifetime if provided with the basic necessities in life and felt safe and secure in their environment. Every person living on this planet should have access to free health care, a comfortable shelter and never worry about going hungry. These are unalienable rights afforded every citizen who honestly contributes to society through a productive career, practice compassion towards all mankind and live within the law. Why should the greed of a few derail the promise made by our forefathers to all Americans, to be able to live life under our inalienable right of freedom and pursuit happiness in return. Maybe we could have an electronic government suggestion box. As voters send over their suggestions and then votes tallied to see if the majority come to a consensus on ideas such as socialized free health care, changing some outdated laws and policy, etc, the federal government could put those changes out for majority vote. If the majority of the voters had a suggestion and the government was able to justify why it wasn't feasible to enact into law, then the GAO needs to present their case to the American people, with a valid reason, as to why it could not implement the idea into law. An example: a 10% income tax across the board to simplify the tax code and eliminate ways for corporations and wealthy individuals to shelter income and reducing their tax liability. If the government calculated that it just wasn't enough revenue to support expenses while minimizing future deficits, then they would have to show how they came up with the calculations so voters could then consider any rebuttals. Then request another call to vote on the initiative based on the proposal that would work.

Chapter 4

A Time For Change Is Now

So how do we get started and energize the good citizens in this nation to finally stand up for those rights given to *all* Americans by our founding fathers.

First, we should change the voting requirements in this country. It should be compulsory that all legal citizens upon turning 18 years of age register to vote in this country.

Second, when a general election is held in this country or call to vote on an initiative by citizens, 51% of the registered voters need to be determined to elect or re-elect a president or adopt new laws. With compulsory voting requirements enacted, failure to record the required percentage of votes for a new or re-elected president or enactment of new laws will easily be determined as null and void during that election or a call-for-vote request. If none of the candidates running for president for the first time, receive the required 51% of the popular votes to be elected, then a secondary list of candidates need to be available for a timely, second attempt to vote a president into office. If the president is up for re-election and doesn't receive 51% of the votes needed to stay in office for a second term and neither do the candidates running against the president, then perhaps a secondary list of candidates can quickly be identified and voted on to try and determine a winner with 51% of the popular votes. This is a very simplified idea to try and at least get people thinking and government officials currently involved in our election process, to present alternative ways of electing our president and allowing laws to be enacted. The new voting laws would be absent the current partisan influence that adversely affects the outcomes of the election process in place today.

Assuming that low turnout is a reflection of disenchantment or indifference, a poll with very low turnout may not be an accurate reflection of the will of the people. On the other hand, if low turnout is a reflection of contentment of voters about likely winners or changes to the law, then low turnout is as legitimate as high turnout, as long as the right to vote exists.

Compulsory voting

One of the strongest factors affecting voter turnout is whether voting is compulsory. In Australia, voter registration and attendance at a polling booth have been mandatory since the 1920s. These rules are strictly enforced, and the country has one of the world's highest voter turnouts. Several other countries have similar laws, generally with somewhat reduced levels of enforcement. If a Bolivian voter fails to participate in an election, the citizen may be denied withdrawal of their salary from the bank for three months. In Mexico and Brazil, existing sanctions for non-voting are minimal or are rarely enforced. When enforced, compulsion has a dramatic effect on turnout.

With intentional gerrymandering of districts by conservatives, restrictive voting practices at the polls enacted by conservatives and the losers not accepting defeat, the voting public has all but lost their protections given to everyone equally under the Constitution of The United States of America. With politics removed from our rule of governance in this country, the risk of rigging the system in favor of one candidate over another is greatly reduced, if not completely eliminated. This would now allow scam artists to come up with a new and improved way to try and pull the wool over the eyes of the voters. Back to work boys on C Street!

Chapter 5

Cleanup On Aisle 4......

O k, now it is time to change the face of government in this country and let the citizens decide what is best for Americans instead of self-serving or ineffective politicians assuring us that they are the only ones who are qualified to know what we need and want as a society overall.

I therefore think it would be an honorable and appropriate gesture to allow those elected officials who continue to commit crimes against all humanity and abuse their once respected positions while in public service, to voluntarily resign from office without prejudice. Most politicians in Congress have the financial resources to retire from office without any negative impact on their quality of life. The politicians who have always tried to do right by the American people and want to continue to work for the people will not be challenged to resign their current positions in Congress. If lawmakers have consistently voted against helping the good people of America or have any documented ties to special interest groups and they refuse to leave office voluntarily then they should be dealt with privately and outside the immunity protections given to them while on the job. The evil doers know who they are and we the people know who they are and strongly recommend they do the honorable thing and leave office quickly and never be heard from again. Otherwise they can defend their actions before a jury of their piers, at their own expense, for the harm inflicted on others by acting outside the code of ethics they swore to uphold upon entering office.

Did you know that you can sue anyone for any reason in the private sector? Not being in the legal profession or understanding liability laws in this country beyond the layman's interpretation of what they mean, I still know the right of a private citizen to try and seek relief through the legal system if they feel they suffered a personal loss due to the actions of another person or person's. This is a basic right of all citizens of this country. Attorneys have made sure of that right. From there, and once turned over to the legal professionals, the outcome with a cause of action could end up just about anywhere.

Let me give you a case in point. I worked as Customer Service Manager for a non-profit agency, that provided weatherization measures for dwellings primarily owned or rented by low income participants applying for assistance. I would supervise crews of workers to go out to dwellings where the occupants qualified for certain energy efficient measures to be retrofitted into their homes through the program, while at no cost to them as homeowners or their landlords if the applicants were renters. New double pane windows, new entry doors, weather stripping, attic insulation, would be installed by crews of primarily Latino workers in this case, since that was the predominant population of residents in the town our agency was licensed in. The work the crews performed in the homes had to follow a strict set of standards that complied with all building code requirements and completed work was inspected on a regular bases by the state. I rarely had any issues with the Latino workers but did have repeated issues with one of the Caucasian crew leaders not performing satisfactorily in his job as required. After a number of poor reviews over a period of several years I finally had to let him go. Three weeks later I was served papers in a lawsuit he filed against my boss and me as the co-defendant. His claim in the suit was for unlawful termination and one of the causes of action listed was that I personally discriminated against him because he was Caucasian. Are you kidding me? Let's put this into perspective folks. As I said before I was born a financially challenged 'white' child. But more important than that I was born a Caucasian in Texas! To put this in perspective and to anyone born outside the biggest state in the world, I was actually considered an 'extra white' child by state standards! So, for this disgruntled, ex-employee Caucasian with swastikas tattooed all over his arms to accuse me, an 'extra white' member of the Caucasian race, of discriminating against him while favoring the 'home boys' more, get out of here! In my deposition and once the plaintiff's attorney stopped smirking in between reading the discrimination claim brought against me, he would keep asking me what I had against the white race. I told him that I discriminated against his client for not performing satisfactorily in his job as described in the job description. His performance reviews showed little improvement with adequate warnings so I had just cause to terminate his employment with the agency. The plaintiff and his attorney knew all along they had no case so settled early on, but only after disrupting my life in the process.

Members of Congress have provided immunity for themselves against any potential negative outcomes associated with legislation they voted on while in session. The current gun laws voted in by Congress provide members immunity against prosecution regardless of any negative outcome from the bill being signed into law. That is why many members of Congress show no remorse for the horrific event that took place at Sandy Hook Elementary School where so many children lost their lives needlessly. They are indemnified against any unforeseen consequences by their participation in debating a bill later signed into law. That said though, why does the intentional shutdown of the federal government last year provide the same immunity to those lawmakers responsible for such an egregious act as they still enjoy while doing their work in Congress? Every American, who was harmed by the misdeeds of a few deranged lawmakers through their intentional shut down of the government last year, should be compensated for their losses. Since it apparently cannot be done publically then I would look into private sector remedies. Perhaps if you were one of the thousands of workers furloughed from your job during the shutdown and never compensated for lost wages or other income don't you think someone needs to be held accountable for this intentional and malicious act? There must be some law firms who specialize in class-action law suits interested in pursuing a case such as this further. Maybe it is too late at this point. I would think just the threat of a private lawsuit against those individuals in Congress who signed the list supporting the shutdown would start to shake things loose in a now dysfunctional body of government. Most are attorneys anyway so they know how disruptive lawsuits can be to peoples' lives. Maybe a few of the prime offenders of obstruction would quietly resign so we could begin to clear the way for the remaining members plus new ones coming in who would honestly like to get back to the business at hand. For all I know members of Congress may have given themselves blanket immunity against anything they do on or off the job. Diplomatic immunity while residing in your own country?

President Obama's administration is very capable of running the government and protecting the citizens of this great country from any outside harm until the decision is made with how to start restructuring Congress so that our current partisan malfeasance does not proliferate any further. Members of Congress have been MIA over the past 4-5 years anyway so what's another couple of years of inactivity while the institution is revamped for the next president coming in.

Positive change will not happen overnight and we all need to work together with compassion and consideration for our fellow citizens if we want to make a difference. In a democratic society such as ours, the right to vote our personal beliefs is the only legitimate avenue for each and every one of us to have a voice in government collectively. The other option being suggested by some of our current leaders in government is to arm every American citizen and potentially use force to bring about change. That is a pretty extreme political platform to be running on and certainly a slippery slope to be heading down. I personally think most Americans would like to try peaceful and compassionate means for change before arming grandma with an M-16 and sending her to the store on her fortified and combat ready Rascal scooter!

Chapter 6

How This Will Not Work

1. Feel as you currently do that you are only one person and certainly can have no impact on change by yourself. Besides it is much easier to just complain about how bad things are than to actually try and gather support for change and expend any of your own energy to benefit yourself and others in the process.

2. Not really believing that the 'will of the people' is a fundamental right given to everyone wishing to live free through compassion and goodwill towards all mankind.

3. Not believing in yourself or your ability to find purpose to your life on this planet.

4. Content with your life the way it is and really don't have the time or ambition to get involved.

5. Not having a basic understanding that change is a slow process and it must be enacted in an orderly and systematic manner. This is not an a-la-carte menu where you can pick and choose what you personally want through change. In other words, if you want that day off to go to a concert then you have to make a positive contribution to help stabilize the economy by performing in your job to the best of your ability. No more slackers, even if your employer does not recognize the contributions you make to a productive work environment. If you are not challenged in life

to do your personal best, move on, but do not hold up the line at the buffet! There is a systematic and methodical approach that needs to happen with any positive change brought about. There are no shortcuts in life unfortunately if you are searching for a positive outcome with some purpose.

6. Having too much to lose if the current system is changed so will stop at nothing to derail the will of the people. Conservative politicians, corporations and wealthy individuals seem content with the status quo in Washington, even though their campaign for change would actually erase some of the gains they achieved through the current administrations policies.

7. If you do not act with your conscience but instead make choices based on false beliefs and perceived populous ideals. I think the majority of the Tea Party followers are being manipulated through fear and not able to make rational decisions. You have to ask yourself, why would supporters at the Tea Party rallies, most already on some government subsidies, want their lifeline eliminated as some political leaders are advocating for? Question the real motives behind another persons' rhetoric when it challenges your individual beliefs and ideals.

8. Having no compassion for other living beings on this planet. If it is all about you, this definitely does not fit into your personal agenda in life.

9. Unable to accept any responsibility for your own actions. Many people go through life thinking that when things go wrong and they are personally harmed in any way, it always has to be someone else's fault. This false belief is at times reinforced by attorneys trying to defend your claim that you were actually harmed in any way by the negligent act of someone else. Do you remember the story of the woman who spilled hot coffee on her lap after being handed her order through the drive-up window of the restaurant? She was 100% responsible for the accident yet attorneys advised her of her to try and blame someone else for the unfortunate situation and hold them responsible. This type

of greed and misuse of the justice system to benefit a few only provides ammunition for those feeling they really do not ever have to take responsibility for their own actions since there will always be someone else around to defend their actions.

10. Taking little initiative of your own to understand when a statement is taken out of context that it has no basis in fact or truth but instead, is simply conjecture. For instance, the claim by the NRA that it is everyone's right under the Second Amendment to the Constitution for individuals to purchase and carry firearms of choice for personal protection. This claim has no validation described in the Charters of Freedom and Democracy to support it as fact based, but rather is solely a marketing ploy by this organization to promote gun sales through intentional misinterpretation of the law. It is a dangerous precedence when someone speaks out of context but even greater consequences result when the listener misinterprets the message to be factual. Another example is the criticism of the president for not turning the economy around fast enough. Those critical of his tireless efforts to go it alone, on everything he does, are simply shifting the focus away from the fact that they are doing nothing to help the situation but instead only contributing to the slow turnaround perceived by the public. It takes one to two minutes to review online just how many jobs President Obama has created over the past 5 or so years and how many more would have been recorded if the obstructionists in Congress would do their job and help the cause instead of always throwing up roadblocks to progress. This is not rocket science folks! If you really want to believe that everything wrong in the world today is one mans fault then whatever obstacles you face moving ahead from this point forward are yours and yours alone to overcome. Those you supported to further their agenda under the guise of looking out for your best interests, will certainly not be anywhere to be found when you go looking for them to return the favor in your time of need. Hey 'tan man' from Ohio, hey 'Mr Peepers' from Kentucky, remember me I had your back when you needed my support? Hello, any Republican lawmakers home? I could use a little help over here!

11. ALLOW SPECIAL INTERESTS THROUGH THEIR CONSERVATIVE 'MASTERS OF SPIN' TRY AND CONVINCE YOU THIS CANNOT POSSIBLY WORK. AFTER ALL, HOW COULD COMMON CITIZENS HAVE ANY IDEA OF THE COMPLEXITIES OF GOVERNMENT AND INDUSTRY TO SIMPLY VOTE CHANGE AND EXPECT IT TO HAPPEN BECAUSE IT IS THEIR WILL. AS STATED BEFORE, THE NAYSAYERS WILL PULL OUT EVERY RESOURCE THEY HAVE TO MAKE A CASE AGAINST 'WE THE PEOPLE' EVEN TRYING TO TAKE CONTROL OF OUR UNALIENABLE RIGHT TO VOTE FOR THE FREEDOMS GIVEN TO ALL AMERICAN CITIZENS BY OUR FOREFATHERS UNDER THE CONSTITUTION. INDUSTRY LEADERS AND THE POLITICIANS AND LOBBYISTS THEY FUND WILL USE EVERY FEAR TACTIC IMAGINABLE TO TRY AND BRAINWASH PEOPLE AND MANIPULATE THE TRUE CAUSE SO THEY CAN GUARANTEE THEIR CONTINUED DOMINANCE IN A FREE MARKET.

IF YOU ALLOW THOSE DRIVEN BY MONEY AND GREED TO WIN THEN YOU NEED TO ACCEPT FULL RESPONSIBILITY FOR THE FATE AND POTENTIAL PERIL OF ALL FUTURE GENERATIONS TRYING TO EXIST ON THIS PLANET. IF YOUR CONSCIENCE TELLS YOU THIS IS THE RIGHT THING TO DO BUT ARE TOO WEAK TO STAND BEHIND YOUR CONVICTIONS THEN YOU HAVE A MORAL IMPERATIVE TO TALK TO YOUR CHILDREN AND GRANDCHILDREN. YOU NEED TO APOLIGIZE NOW AND ASK TO BE FORGIVEN BECAUSE YOU WERE TOO WEAK OR APATHETIC TO TRY AND PROVIDE SOME ASSURANCES TO THEM THAT THEIR LIFE ON THIS PLANET WOULD BE HEALTHLY AND SAFE NOT ONLY DURING THEIR LIFETIME BUT FOR THEIR CHILDRENS LIFETIME TOO.

Chapter 7

Oversight? Oversight!
I Don't Havta Provide No Stinkin' Oversight!

So government, stay out of my business and stop regulating industry and stop providing consumer protection because it is stalling growth in the economy. Industry knows what is best for their shareholders. Who does the government think they are telling coal burning power plant owners how to regulate their harmful emissions. They have never had any issues in the past with residents living around the plants complaining that it was hard to breathe or anything like that. The verdict is still out on just how much of a negative impact carbon emissions have on say, climate change. Industry is monitoring what they are doing but if for any reason there happens to be an 'accident' during the routine course of business, someone will clean it up, don't ya worry. If the damage created by the industry suddenly becomes irreversible because the harmful by-products produced by their plants were improperly monitored, then the principals of the business are probably betting that future generations can try and mitigate any catastrophic fallout caused as a result of the prevailing attitude of the times, while always claiming that it wasn't their fault to begin with.

How would the government know what to do any better than BP in the event of another oil spill like what happened in the Gulf awhile back? Or who knows best how to control the harmful by-products that run off of coal fired power plants like the one run by Duke Energy in North Carolina. Apparently not Duke because of the most recent discovery in North Carolina where three of their power plants have been dumping tons of toxic coal ash for years into rivers and streams that feed potable water supplies in the area. The governor of that state, a previous employee of Duke Energy, said federal regulators did not need to monitor the power plants because he had it under control through his own state run agency.

The one thing that federal regulators have going for them that industry does not recognize as being a crucial part of their business model is 'prevention.' Bottom line in a company usually trumps safety when convincing shareholders that the 'principals' in the business know how best to contain costs in order to maximize profits. Besides, that is why they have liability insurance just in case the unexpected happens and property or the environment is damaged or worse yet, loss of lives due solely to their negligence. Insurance underwriters have their back, who has yours?

Most man-made destruction recorded can be traced back to the origin of the problem that caused the devastation in the first place. Once the cause of problem is identified, more often than not it is concluded that it was preventable! This is one more example of the sad state of affairs that we as a society realize when the attitudes of a few in our country and the world for that matter, believes wealth today trumps ignorance in knowing that their misdeeds today will certainly contribute to the ultimate destruction of our planet in the not too distant future. But let's get our priorities straight people, its more important for the elite members of our society to be able to purchase another Swiss watch or designer clothes or another fancy car to satisfy their insatiable appetite for material things than it is to worry about the continued strife so many people face today just trying to exist, much less being harmed through no fault of their own.

The previous administrations attitude about government regulation of industry allowed the following events to occur solely due to a lack of internal oversight and questionable safety practices being ignored. Each and every one of the following occurrences could have been mitigated or even prevented if an established public regulatory agency could have intervened and monitored the safety and security practices of those businesses who choose to ignore any outside oversight.

- Terrorists attack on American Soil on 9/11

- Big banks, U.S. automakers, airlines, Wall Street, mortgage lenders, home builders either failed or had to be reorganized to remain in business due to the deliberate malfeasance by these industry leaders rejecting performance guidelines by government regulators. All previous requirements for a borrower to qualify for a mortgage loan to purchase a home were circumvented by an administration anxious to portray a robust economy actually on the verge of collapse. Bush II used to boast that under his watch home ownership was a reality for more people than ever before. It was a win-win for banks and Wall Street and a lose-lose for individuals purchasing homes, plus the monumental loss to the economy overall. Mission accomplished!

- Largest financial crises since the Great Depression

- Largest loss of lives and property damage in our nation's history from flooding due to inadequate levies and poor response from FEMA personnel in the aftermath of Hurricane Katrina.

- Biggest spike in gasoline prices in our nation's history as a result of intentional manipulation of prices by commodity traders. Boys will be boys sometimes.

- Largest drop in personal wealth on a global scale since the Great Depression due to Wall Street being allowed to self-regulate their creative investment portfolios. What's a derivative again?

- Largest increase in health insurance premiums on record.

- Largest percentage in personal bankruptcies in American history.

- Largest number of documented suicides attributed directly to the collapse of the economy.

- Greatest number of consumer product recalls and food safety violations on record due to the federal agencies in charge of consumer protections being downsized or budgets being drastically cut only to minimize their effectiveness.

- All commercial aircraft grounded for the first in aviation history immediately following attack on 9/11, with the exception of Saudi residents in the country at the time. Everyone of Saudi descent was allowed to leave the country immediately for their own protection. From what? Since all other air travel was suspended in and out of the country at least those of Middle Eastern descent did not have to wait long for a flight out of the United States.

- Lenders ignored any previously mandated usury laws by enacting predatory lending practices assuring borrowers could never repay the mortgage loan they secured on their homes.

These are some of the factors contributing to the Great Recession that President Obama inherited when entering office in 2008. So when people say this president has been slow to turn the economy around from the brink of collapse and since taking office, his record of creating jobs month after month with no support from some members of Congress, is worthy of a medal of honor and achievement, not condemnation. But lets not inflate his ego too much by giving him credit for his accomplishments against the wishes of the 'blamers' in Congress. Or maybe the naysayers are the true 'Dreamers' who congregate together to hope and pray for a better time when a person of color is not running the country.

Chapter 8

Let's Get Started

The first thing, 'we the people' need to do is all try and turn out to vote in the upcoming elections. Even if it means traveling great distances or standing in long lines to have your voice heard in government, it has to be done. As I said before, after the wealthy donors have spent great sums of money to try and buy the outcome with elections, show them that the will of the people will not be diminished by their futile attempts to suppress the right of all American's voices to be heard. Tell them that your convictions and beliefs are yours alone and not for sale at any price. Always stand up for what you think is right for yourself as an individual and take pride in what you stand for, knowing that if you sell your principals for some promised short term gain, eventually you will be asking a higher power for forgiveness for being so weak and causing unnecessary harm to yourself and those around you.

Once the smoke clears and the good people of this nation realize that government can work alongside all citizens by providing support needed to enrich our own lives and lead each of us to a more fulfilling existence. Starting the process for change is always the most difficult thing for most humans to do. Our comfort zone feels safe because the space we move around in is small and familiar and even if it is not ideal, the unknown with change is just too terrifying for many lacking the self-confidence necessary to get them through it. Our government, through its numerous outreach agencies once provided that support for America's citizens to explore new things and take a chance in life. Whether it was to start a business or go to college, agencies were there to provide some form of support to citizens seeking it. I remember when I started my company around 1970 and the Small Business Administration was there for me to help establish a line-of-credit at my bank so I could have the funds available for day to day operating expenses until the company could begin to sustain itself. They were anxious to provide any support they could to see me succeed with challenging my innovative spirit, contributing to the overall growth of the economy, but most importantly I would be starting a new enterprise that many viewed at the time as the founding principal for what we as a free society truly stood for. Ones ambition leads to ones success then what follows innovation is heralded as 'made in America with pride.' Greed and self-preservation were not the prevailing attitudes in the society I grew up in. Unfortunately today these are the main drivers behind an economy unable to move any faster and resume the lead in our rapidly changing global environment that America once enjoyed by being recognized as the leader in innovation. Political leaders, specifically conservative members of Congress, have wasted our precious time on this planet far too long with their status quo, and even reverse course attitudes. Other developing nations have already passed us up through their innovation and technological advances because they know to remain competitive on a global scale requires a progressive agenda instead of a stagnant one as we in this country are now seeing. For all those out there who need to blame someone for the stagnant growth seen in our economy today, blame yourself for trying to inflict your personal beliefs on others while supporting members of Congress who put their self serving agenda ahead of doing what is right for the country. Obviously a lose-lose proposition for everyone in the end!

The process to change the current system of electing individuals to public office based solely on their political affiliations will not be easy by any sense of the imagination. The only three choices available to voters today is conservative leaning, progressive leaning and middle of the road or progservatives. The issue though is that the universe is made up of individuals who have a right to co-exist among like species and practice their beliefs, personal convictions and ideals, but only if on a personal level. If your elected official has similar beliefs and convictions as you do, get together for a cup of coffee with them and high-five each other until the sun comes down but don't expect that public servant to use their positions of power to preach the gospel according to you two, with everyone else. It is not in their job description and you have no right to try and mandate change for everyone based on your own personal convictions. Got it! So now, we the rest of the people, have to expend unnecessary energy to clean up the mess due solely to the abuse of power by a few in the once honored branch of government created to represent all citizens instead of just the wealthy and influential factions.

In the private sector, upper management has to build a strong case in support of terminating employment of a non-performing employee. The system currently favors the employee over the employer so due diligence is required for a company to fire an employee even if there is exhaustive documentation that the worker was not doing the job they were hired to do within work standards expected of them. Since members of Congress apparently report to no one and have no code of conduct for their performance on the job, it is going to be a bit more difficult to get the 'coasters' out. Not impossible though as some lawmakers are relying on this false sense of immunity protection, to discourage anyone from trying. Maybe during the transition away from party affiliation, now synonymous with qualifications when electing public officials, every candidate running for office can be listed as Independent. Speaking of Independents, I recently read that millennials are starting to shift their societal attitudes towards the more middle of the road approach to politics. If you are still not that sure of your own ability to change things in a progressive atmosphere then middle of the road is a good first step in the right direction. Most people today firmly believe that staying where we are or going backwards is no longer an option.

Those on the far right and far left are so idealistic in their beliefs that it becomes pointless to even think they can ever imagine anything differently, much less change their point of view in any way. If people want to support Senator Rand Paul for president in 2016 because of his current talking points then don't complain when thing don't go as expected if he gets elected into office. Remember this is guy not that long ago who believed private business owners had the right to segregate patrons, entering the premises, based solely on the proprietors personal beliefs and convictions. Beliefs like those of Senator Paul are rooted so deeply into the character of an individual that this deep moral conviction can resurface at any time. Though I still believe people can change their attitudes and I hope Senator Paul has, but don't vote for someone just because you are disillusioned with the perceived performance of one party over another. Especially don't vote for someone because you are offended by Obama and democrats for hacking into your emails! Unlike Bush II, a Republican, who started the eavesdropping law after 9/11, and rumored to scan personal emails while sitting back in one of the rooms of color in the White House over a six pack of his favorite brew, precludes such activity by our current president outside of any national security threats. Anyway, have something to hide mister? My point is research the background of any candidate before making your final determination if they are really the best candidate for the job. I think 'none of the above' is definitely going to need to be on the ballots in the future, but only if those already in office have term limits with their tenure in office. I stopped taking the local paper shortly after the election in 2012 because the Editorial Board endorsed Romney for president, solely on the fact that he wasn't Barack Obama! Give me a break. Not one substantive reason why Romney was more qualified to run the country than Obama.

Moving forward with 'House Cleaning,' if you can think of any harm that has come to you, your family or friends as a direct result of a public official acting outside the scope of duties they swore to uphold while in office, then ask around with other members of your community, especially any in the legal profession, if they think you have a case in the private sector against those who willfully and intentionally abused their positions of power to hurt unsuspecting citizens. I would hope after this book is released, that some law firms specializing in class-action status will step forward to build a case against those who perpetrated these acts against all humanity. American's should demand that the Justice Department look further into criminal charges against some, who abused their positions in Congress while admitting to taking bribes only to manipulate the outcome of voting on a piece of legislation brought to the floor. I really doubt that charges of racketeering against a member of Congress affords them the blanket immunity from criminal prosecution they believe they should have while performing the work they swore to uphold upon entering office.

If we as a society continue down the path of unspoken acceptance with a practice because it is something 'commonly done by most' and recognized to be the only interpretation of the law, then it just further validates that we as a culture need take no responsibility for our actions. Everyone drives faster than the posted speed limit and ignores traffic laws, is it now considered acceptable behavior because it is such common practice? John Boehner admitted to accepting bribes from Big Oil to influence the outcome of a piece of legislation being voted on by members on the floor of the House. Is that now considered legal standing since the Speaker said it is 'common practice' by him personally and by other members of Congress. Until we differentiate between 'rule of law' as it applies to the rich and powerful and the remaining members of society, can we continue down our current path where the perpetrators of a crime continue to accept no responsibility for their actions, just because they can? If you continually run red lights or stop signs while driving and the police are never around to cite you for the violations, then I guess your unlawful behavior becomes excepted practice, at least in your mind which is all that matters. That is until someone else is harmed through your negligent behavior. Of course if you find a good attorney your defense could then be that you thought running red lights or stop signs was legal since you were never cited in the past to indicate otherwise. It has now become a harsh reality within our societal values that people don't need to assume any personal responsibility for their own actions or inactions and by providing public acknowledgement to the contrary, remains a dangerous precedence going forward.

Let's put this in perspective, say Congress votes to allow Big Oil to self-regulate safety inspections on their oil rigs out in the ocean because lawmakers were influenced to vote that way. Then there is an explosion on the oil rig due to a faulty valve that should have been replaced during a routine safety inspection but overlooked because inspectors were trying to keep operating expenses down. Numerous lives were lost and the impact to the environment was catastrophic due to the crude oil flowing into the waterways. Should members of

Congress who voted in favor of self-inspections on oil rigs assume any responsibility for this preventable accident? Lawmakers certainly would not see their role in allowing the accident to occur, so it was obviously someone else's fault, right? If a private citizen makes a deliberate choice in their life that ends up having a negative impact on another person, the chain of events leading up to that consequential outcome could be investigated to lead back to the person responsible for the catastrophe in the first place. The perpetrator can claim it was never their intention for that outcome to occur, but it still should not exempt them from their participation in what ultimately led to needless harm being inflicted on another person through their association in the matter. I may be naïve to the subtleties of the law but to the layperson this has all the appearances of a double standard within the rule of law that governs all people in our nation. People need to take a stand and question these contradictions when challenging our core beliefs, and the foundation for which all laws governing the citizens in this country are based upon. Otherwise as you put your head between your legs and grab that seat cushion as your floatation device, may heaven help us all if this prevailing attitude continues to guide us through the downward spiral we now find ourselves as a civilization moving towards our eventual extinction.

On a more positive note and as the governments' house starts to return to some sense of order, lets start to think of ways to streamline our governments' role in providing quality services to its citizens in return for a more productive and content society that builds on the strength of 'Made in America by Americans.' By removing the impetus by some in Washington to lead through greed and corruption, hopefully branches and agencies within the government can return to the job they were created to perform in the first place. Some of the Scandinavian countries are stellar examples showing how self-sufficient economies can coexist in the global arena only when the societies are defined by the attitudes that collectively contribute to equality and good will for all its citizens. Those contradictions with our moral and societal beliefs that continue to undermine the ability to come together as a once caring and compassionate society, because of the loss in trust with those around us, needs to be remedied before positive change can come about in America. Attitudes about guns, equal rights, government spending and waste, safety nets for the disadvantaged, basic needs guaranteed for all citizens like healthcare, housing and food. No one individual has a right to pass judgment on another living creature born to an inalienable right to live a safe and secure existence while on planet earth. Wealth alone does not give anyone the exalted power to pass judgment on others while attempting to diminish their standing in our society as anything other than equal among all living creatures.

Once the government waste is under control, the economy starts to turn around, companies are more profitable and hiring again and the federal deficit is turned into a surplus with subsidized healthcare for every non-obstructionist citizen, then we can vote on a four day work week. Companies need to pay a living wage to all employees. This may be a good opportunity to reevaluate compensation packages for every classification of employee. I personally do not think any employee should be paid more than $250,000 annually. An individual can live quite comfortably on even $100,000 a year. If public companies and institutions were not compensating some, with unimaginable salaries and bonuses, then there would be a more equitable distribution of earnings for all workers while continuing to have no effect on the bottom line as a result.

We need to bring manufacturing back to this country to create more jobs and be able to proudly purchase goods with the emblem "Made in America" once again. We have the resources, the technology and the labor force to be completely self-sufficient within our own borders. The only problem is we cannot afford to purchase our own goods at the current cost of labor and materials in this country alongside the unsustainable earnings distribution seen in the workplace. It is the huge disparity in salaries that has prevented all workers from earning at least a living minimum wage. As long as all workers are compensated for the skill level they perform under then the cost to manufacture goods could be reduced and companies could sell their products to more Americans. We are forced to purchase just about everything we want and some things we need, from China or India because their labor costs are so much less than ours.

I have a solution that will stimulate manufacturing in this country, close the trade deficit and be able to become less dependent on foreign made goods to supply our insatiable need for material things. If the basic necessities to live a comfortable life were made available to everyone then discretionary spending would still flourish by everyone making an acceptable living wage. For individuals receiving greater compensation for their job performances consistently above and beyond the expectations listed in the job description, they would have the discretionary reserves to purchase those things considered luxury items to most people. Seniors remain an untapped resource who give migrant workers a run for their money, no pun intended, because of the ability to learn tasks quickly while expecting only modest compensation in return for their contributions to a productive workforce. Remember though sonny, we are good to go as long as there is no offset with our Social Security checks because of any additional earnings we may receive. Since the majority of the Tea Party members are on government subsidies we could require these welfare recipients, if not totally disabled, to work for their subsidy and/or housing allowance unless they choose to join our democratic society instead of continuing to oppose it. We could employ migrant workers, pay them a living wage as long as they have citizenship status or applied for citizenship in this country, to work in jobs other Americans choose not to do. Once we are able to lower labor costs, manufacture our own goods then more people will get jobs earning a living wage and be able to buy products "Made in America," instead of going outside our borders to support other economies. Companies need to get away from this mentality that the only way to recruit qualified personnel for higher level positions is to pay exorbitant salaries and provide golden parachutes. There are more than enough qualified workers to fill any position hundreds of times over and willing to meet performance goals while working for a lower wage. The board of directors of companies should be made up of ordinary citizens to provide the necessary oversight when setting compensation packages for all positions. These citizen review boards, just like those part of the federal government would oversee and provide recommendations that benefit every one not just a few select individuals.

I think an article written in the American Scholar by William Deresiewicz pretty much sums up one of the compelling reasons I am writing this book: "We have a crises of leadership in America because our overwhelming power and wealth, earned under earlier generations of leaders, made us complacent, and for too long we have been training leaders who only know how to keep the routine going. Who can answer questions but do not know how to ask them. Who can fulfill goals but don't know how to set them. Who think about how to get things done, but not whether they're worth doing in the first place. What we have now are the greatest technocrats the world has ever seen, people who have been trained to be incredibly good at one specific thing, but who have no interest in anything beyond their area of expertise. What we don't have are people who can think for themselves, people who can formulate a new way of doing things, a new way of looking at things: people with vision. Introspection means talking to yourself, acknowledge things to yourself."

This attitude and way of thinking that surrounds true introspection as a means to assimilate greater knowledge and apply it in a meaningful way with everything we do in life, represents my own personal views to finding purpose in ones own existence on the planet.

As I said above, creativity and innovation are truly lacking in today's society. Our imaginations have been suppressed because those in power do not want us to think on our own. Their belief in mankind is that "a mind is a dangerous thing." Join me in proving them wrong and start to bring interest and innovation back into our lives during our brief time on this planet. I have always believed in the old adage: "THE MEEK SHALL INHERIT THE EARTH!" Creativity and innovation are essential to be able to engage the younger generation and have them start to 'buy in' with making their lives purposeful on this planet. Creativity and innovation are essential to having a productive and collaborative workforce crossing all generational, gender and ethnic barriers. That is why I so firmly believe in focusing more on job creation through space exploration as a viable and attainable goal towards solving many of the inequities and shortcomings facing the current and future generation of thinkers and doers.

Prologue

I have already lived an enriched and purposeful life. Personally, I have nothing to lose or gain if my fellow Americans have no aspirations to try and do the same. All I can do is strongly recommend you try it because I think you may like the ultimate gratification realized, because during the brief passage on this planet you discovered your purpose in being who you are and what you are capable of becoming. The fulfillment of ones dreams and ambitions, always believing in your ability to be the best of the best at what ever you choose to do throughout life while striving to have a positive impact on those around you, is a testament to the true meaning of life as I see it.

The measure of success for me personally is not with the amount of material things my wife and I have accumulated over time, even though that does provide us with a greater sense of security and comfort through the remainder of our lives, but something only ascertained by me and me alone. I have to say though, I am really attached to my party ice machine and maybe some of my power tools, that's it! If I really had to give up everything else tangible in life except my wife, I could do so knowing that the person I am today and the enriched life I have lead through my worldly travels and successful endeavors pursued, makes me feel complete. The true meaning of life for me today, confirms my thinking early on in my youth, explore your dreams and ambitions always internalizing, what if you tried for yourself, and more importantly what if you did it your way. The knowledge you assimilate within becomes your foundational power to overcome most obstacles put before you throughout your lifetime.

I have now and always will believe in the inherit good in all mankind. We as humans are all a product of our upbringings and the environment in which we grew up in. Life for every living creature on this planet is truly about survival of the fittest. Even if you play by all the rules while exhibiting a spirit of compassion and generosity to those around you, there will always be some lost souls among us trying to take advantage of the good will we try and practice towards everyone alike. Those taking advantage of my caring spirit over the years and who perceived my honorable selfless intentions as a sign of weakness to be exploited for their personal gain, are hopefully in a better place somewhere in the universe by now. I am convinced that those with immense wealth and power for the most part, have taken advantage of the good people of this planet, only to further their insatiable quest for more wealth and power at the expense of a society now lacking in trust of all mankind. The prevailing emotion driving the attitudes of people today rests solely on fear. People living in fear will always remain helplessly subservient to those in power. Those individuals focused solely on the self-serving quest for greater wealth and power can always rely on the weakness of others to further their own ambitions.

I would like to make the following plea to all the fine public service officials who took an oath of office to uphold the 'will of the people' first and foremost while in their positions in office: Internalize between right and wrong, good and evil and conclude as you must that the current 'rules of law' that provide the foundation for the attitudes and behavior necessary to maintain a free and democratic way of governance, are no longer in the image of our founding fathers and no longer work for those living in our ever changing society today.

Those tireless crusaders in Congress who have worked for the will of the people over any self or outside interests should stay the course knowing that help may be on the way if the American spirit, built on the care and compassion towards all others, is awakened once again. Once the institution established by our forefathers is cleansed of the evil doers. Perhaps through compulsory voting, the will of the majority of Americans can finally be realized by voting in philanthropic and humanitarian individuals to play an important role in reshaping our government in the eyes of its citizenry.

I have suggested throughout this book, that we are now at an impasse in this country and need to decide collectively if we want to reset the way we choose public officials to run our government or remain complacent and disconnected with the reality of the crises continuing to tear at the symbol with what this great nation was built on – "I AM PROUD TO BE AN AMERICAN." Newcomers to this country may be able to chant those words without really understanding what they mean, but those of us who have been around for awhile only to witness the intentional dismantling of a once caring society by just a small number of lost souls, can now only whisper those words "I am proud to be an American" in private.

People today need not even question their moral convictions to understand that the drafters of the Articles of Freedom and Democracy reminded all of us that our duty as free citizens requires: whenever any *form of government* becomes destructive of these ends, it is the *right of the people* to alter or abolish it, and to institute new *government,* laying its foundation on such principals and organizing its powers in such form, as to them shall seem most likely to effect their *safety and happiness.*

The time has come to energize the progressives in this country and take a stand against all those trying to diminish the right of equality inherent in all Americans. It is through a few, with their insatiable quest for greater wealth and power that if allowed to go unchecked, will ultimately turn this nation into an oligarchy form of rule. For those needing a party affiliation to move forward lets narrow it down to one, the party of "No More". No more suppressing the rights of the middle class. No more controlling the direction this country is moving without consent of the majority. No more manipulation of the truth by the media attempting only to highlight our weaknesses over our strengths. No more empty rhetoric without substantive dialogue to engage others to question the truth behind what is spoken. If you are unable to argue a case for your ideas then keep them to yourself. No more wasting our precious time on this planet with decision makers acting outside the interest of the majority of Americans. No more allowing one human being to inflict harm on another simply because they got away with it in the past.

Well saddle up and hold on for a wild ride elite and powerful. Take your material spoils you've acquired without compassion for the human suffering you have caused so many through your acts of unkindness. Vanish quietly from a society who no longer looks up to you as our once respected role models. Your previous entertaining antics are coming to an end as the American people can now move forward in anticipation of a new season of our favorite TV series returning in the fall. I for one have paid my fair share of income taxes for many years during my career only to feel a deep and depressing sense of buyer's remorse today. I feel we have a share of ownership in America greater than that of the wealthy elite and corporations based here, because unlike those groups, most people respect their obligation to support a system that returns some of the proceeds back to its citizens. Unfortunately, most American's are feeling shortchanged today because the return on our investment with the government has become so marginal. Although I do appreciate that many of the museums in our nations' capital are still free to go into. I have always abhorred waste and frivolous spending by those who take little or no responsibility for paying their fare share into a system designed to benefit the majority of the people in this nation. Avoiding paying your fair share of income taxes just to purchase another vacation home does not constitute a humanitarian attitude towards your fellow mankind.

About The Author

Writing this book has afforded me an opportunity, for the first time in my life, to step back and reflect. The first thing that comes to mind is, "wow, what a long strange trip it has been." Long because it seems so far in the distant past that I was running my own business or building a home for my wife and I or discovering new career opportunities. Strange in a sense that during my explorations throughout life, while searching for answers to whatever, I never even thought about where my journeys would take me because the end was not my goal, but rather the means in which to achieve the end was what really mattered. I envisioned, before ever breaking ground to pour my first foundation, what my wife and I wanted our dream home to look like, but got so wrapped up in the very long process of actually learning the building trades so I could construct the dwelling, that I did not revisit that thought until the end of the project. I remember after about 25 years into the project saying "Yeah, this actually turned out better than I imagined, give myself a high five," now time to move on!

Every time I tried something new, armed only with the self-confidence in my own ability to jump in without hesitation then consistently surpass my own expectations, it allowed me to dispel any fear in those around me that no harm would come to them as a result their continued support of my crazy ideas. That bond between friends and family was tested time and time again because I never let on that I acted solely on intuition and a strong self-belief in my ability to succeed at whatever I undertook while always being cognizant of the safety and well being of those around me. The days of getting my first muscle car with only a learners permit to drive, to purchasing a racing sailboat before ever understanding that sailing lesions, prior to my maiden voyage on a 16ft catamaran under the Golden Gate Bridge, would have been prudent. Those who participated with me during some of these memorable moments, soon began to seek faith in the universe through a higher power other than I pretended to maintain. None of the willing participants throughout my journey of life ever complained to me that they had any permanent scarring as a result of my frolicking around, although new recruits to share in my adventures were becoming more difficult to find after awhile. I suspect that was due to the writing on the stalls and walls in the public restrooms left at the scene of the last mishap by those claiming to be my true friends, just before abandoning me. I learned from the beginning that during our short passage on planet earth, one should never let fear of the unknown prevent you from living your dreams and aspirations. Because I see such a dramatic cultural change in attitudes today in our society, I have become disheartened that so many people living in fear of the unknown, will never find the courage to follow their dreams as I did throughout my life of enrichment. That is a very sad statement encompassing the direction, we as a once proud nation seem to now be moving.

So who do I think I am throwing out all these fancy words and theories about a better life and what's in it for me? Well, I have absolutely no recognition or standing in the public eye and very little affirmation of my existence in the private world. Although my wife of 35+ years is constantly reminded of my presence today, I have only a few acquaintances that seem to enjoy my company as much as I do theirs but mutually it seems, only for a limited period of time during each encounter. I have thought of a number of scenarios as to why I have no real long term friends in my life now but my feeling is "screw it if they couldn't take a joke". Hey, I got a sailing manual with the boat, its not my fault it went flying overboard on my first trip out. I always brought plenty of mind altering refreshments on our sailing adventures to minimize the fear that my passengers may be expressing with the captains ability to get us home safe.

Seriously, I believe I am a bit of a loner today due to the choices I made in my life. I have been way too preoccupied exploring and living my own life to have any time remaining to do what is required to build long term relationships with anyone other than my wife. Those around me always commented on how obsessive I seemed to be once I committed myself to another adventure in life. To me, I felt more possessed rather than obsessed in what I was doing. Some of the greatest visionary's and creative thinkers throughout history lived fairly reclusive lives. Besides I realized early in life that I could not move forward freely while dealing with other peoples issues because that would only distract me from my insatiable appetite to learn new things. I am doomed from the beginning anyway since I do not like to watch sports. I tried to watch the fishing channel one time but couldn't get behind the whole competitive nature of the sport. In the early days friends were plentiful because we all had one thing in common and that was we liked to get stoned and just hang together, eating a lot. I realize now that I could never run for public office because the opposition would be all over me trying to analyze the foot prints on my birth certificate for confirmation that I must have been born in another country outside the nation of Texas, because only commies don't like sports!

The reason I feel so strongly about my messages in the book is because I have actually lived such a fulfilling life during a time gone by, when societal attitudes were 180 degrees from where they are today. I remain a dreamer today but know that even in my wildest visions, that things will never return to the way they were. I am still hopeful though that they can return to a sense of what was considered 'normal' within the societal values that this nation was built upon. Realistically it will only happen if we as a society of determined individuals acknowledge that it doesn't have to be the way it is, and collectively engage to make things better for everyone. I see the sense of fear and disparity so prevalent in our world today. I also see that it is 100 percent man-made! A tried and true maneuver by some always nets the same results, to say something repeatedly, over a long enough period of time, the sheep will eventually return back to the flock to feel safe again. If you instill fear of the unknown in peoples mind over and over, eventually they will be afraid while never knowing what of. The masters of manipulation, as with some of our current lawmakers, depend on that one emotion, only to further their quest for greater wealth and power. Anything, repeat after me, anything man-made can be un-man-made if there is such an expression.

In support of my personal beliefs while providing some creditability with my suggestions in the book, I now feel that you need to be the judge for yourselves:

My dad bought a franchise in the 1960's for one of the early fast food chain restaurants then starting to pop up everywhere. Unfortunately the restaurant chain had a short life expectancy of about 10 years before going defunct. The chain would have probably been more successful had the founders modeled their operations more in line with what McDonald's did starting in 1955. But they didn't, because they were out of touch with what the public wanted at the time and never quite understood how to stay competitive in a market about to take off beyond belief. My dad kept trying to convince the founders to serve beer with that burger to gain an advantage in the market before the competition thought of it. The restaurant being in such close proximity to Stanford University though prohibited any business from obtaining a liquor license that near to the campus, so not sure to this day why my dad was even pressing the issue. Perhaps it was because he liked beers and burgers himself. I was just a kid in high school at the time so no one would listen to any ideas I may have had about running the business so I just decided to focus on what I could gain from the experience personally. I quickly advanced through different aspects of the operations end of the business thinking at the time it was because I was doing such a great job at every task I was given. In reality though, my rapid climb to the more responsible positions in the business was primarily due to my dad owning the restaurant. Hey, I polished the stainless steel fixtures, and there were a lot of surfaces, better than anyone else did, so there! Even by the strong objections from the manager with my dad showing favoritism as he did, I was able to quickly advance from cleanup, to short order cook, to front counter then to closing during summer break from 10th grade. No drive-thru, so customers would come up to the counter a little testy to start with, expecting a great meal in return for the exhaustive walk from the parking lot they had just made. I learned customer service skills early on and able to apply those later on in my career. I also saved enough money working in the restaurant to buy things I thought I needed more than my parents thought I did, like fancy stereo equipment or a muscle car. Speaking of stereo's, I thought it was so cool during that same period in my life that I had connections through some of my friends whose dads flew for commercial airlines. Those friends looking for some weekend entertainment used their free family passes to fly anywhere the airlines flew. They would take orders for stereo equipment from a bunch of us, fly to Tokyo and pickup state of the art stuff and return with the goods several days later. Even after paying these 'mules', I mean friends, a slight handling fee for their efforts it turned out to be a great deal for everyone except maybe the airlines. Oh well, both airlines that their dads flew for and their dads for that matter are no longer around, so no harm no foul I guess. To this day I still have some really good sounding and good looking Sansui Speakers!

Once I entered into Junior College, I started to look into my future with a different perspective on life. In between protesting the big war at the time and taking a full load, 12 units in college, I went to work as a computer operator for a service bureau in the area working swing shift. Unless you are from my generation, computer operator and service bureau has absolutely no meaning to you I am sure. To make a long story short, most companies at that time and for whatever reason did not have in-house computers to perform what they do today on PC's and through networking. I am not sure how I even got the job because my resume at the time highlighted my only past work experience as being able to fry hamburgers really quick, and that I was a 'people person' because of my customer service skills I learned while appeasing tired and weary customers after their long trek from the parking lot some 200 feet away. Back then though employers were much more open to in-house training programs for new hires to assist them in learning the skill they were hired to do, even while being paid at the same time. Novel idea today! I was able to take the knowledge I learned while running batch computer jobs on mainframe computers to understand what was lacking in the industry in regards to minimizing the amount of downtime we experienced due to hardware failures. Did he just say fhfwofjgoeriegvdsv? Why can't this guy speak English? Sorry, I am revealing my age again. Anyway after being paid to be trained and slowly becoming less challenged in my position at work, I took a serious look at an opportunity that arose to 'be my own boss.' I told you so, we have to stop training these people on our dime, only to have 'em turn around and go somewhere else, those ungrateful employees!

It took awhile for that whole loyalty thing to finally disappear in the workplace before morphing into what we see today as a more compassionate relationship between employee and employer known as At-will employment agreements. If you have not been one of the lucky few to experience this 'cum-by-yah' environment now being adopted by more companies because of those ungrateful employees in the past being taking their free training and running somewhere else, then here is a synopsis of how it works. Employment can be terminated between employee and employer at any time without cause or warning. That is pretty simple. In other words, no more training programs or anything else like living wages, paid leave, cost of living raises, parking spots, etc. Come to work as scheduled, take any abuse your supervisor wishes to inflict on you and do your job plus 5 other ex-employees jobs who have since left. Oh and pay raises are frozen for everyone except upper management personnel due to overall profits being down since the Great Depression. But don't get me wrong, I'm not bitter! Fortunately I was able to take advantage of that free training gig during the golden years when employers actually showed their appreciation when an employee performed at their job above and beyond what was expected of them.

College for me, after getting my fancy Associate of Arts degree, became a challenge to my free spirit always wanting to stop reading and talking and get out and start doing. I was growing anxious to start applying some of that book knowledge into real world practical experiences. Unfortunately, I still had that implant in me from birth that would occasionally send out an annoying signal to my brain reminding me the only way to truly get ahead in life was to get a higher degree from an accredited institution. As the signal became weaker though, before alkaline batteries, I took getting my Associates of Arts Degree in Business as a sign from the universe that I was good to go and able to break free from the confines of higher education. Besides I was quickly forgetting the foreign language I took over the course of 3 semesters because I was unable to carry on a conversation with anyone other than my pharmacist in Latin. Core courses, you gotta love them!

With some help from my dad, I decided to make the leap and go into business for myself. The venture I got involved with was a startup out of Southern California, where the founder developed a high-tech washing machine for cleaning contamination such as smoke particles off of the recording surfaces of removable computer storage devices. Periodic maintenance of these mechanical devices reduced the frequency of the read-write heads from making contact with the 3000 RPM spinning disks. Seems simple, well the process was and it actually worked as I can attest to because of being one of the biggest skeptics for a number of years, next to equipment manufacturers such as IBM and Control Data. It took about five years before industry acceptance of the process was considered beneficial rather than detrimental to prolonging the life of the equipment and safeguarding the integrity of the data on the disk. Yeah! I can move out of parents house now!

With what little money I was able to save during startup of the business and by living with my parents as long as I could before my wife said it was time to start anew with her and moving away from them, I came up with a down payment towards a 3 acre piece of land in rural Los Gatos Mountains. Growing up on the more prestigious side of the tracks during my adolescence, purchasing an undeveloped piece of land with none of the amenities I had grown to appreciate in modern day times, made me stop and ponder. I found myself repeating over and over again to myself, what was I thinking? After serious coaxing from my new bride, and breaking free from the safety net my parents had so graciously provided me for so long, we moved up to the plot of land to start our lives together in uncharted territory. Fortunately we had a van to sleep in but I had to displace my wife each morning so I could drive down the mountain to an office space in town that the business operated out of. I am not sure what my wife did all day while I was at the office but she seemed to entertain herself until I returned home to begin working the land so that we could plan the development of our future habitat together. The first thing I did after putting in the marijuana garden was build an outhouse and design and build a water system so we could eventually take a shower at our own place instead of using the nearby creek to bath or stopping by our neighbors who were all living in trailers at the time. The only structure on the land when we first moved up was a plywood platform 10 feet by 10 feet suspended in a grove of redwood trees and about 8 feet in the air. There was no electricity in the surrounding area so what minimal electric power requirements we had at first were accommodated by the car battery, until I drove to work. Construction projects in the beginning required that I go down to my folks place and make things with power tools there and then bring the finished materials back up the mountain to install. Eventually we got a generator but only after I built several outbuildings and a totally functional treehouse. I learned from Roy Underhill of The Woodright's Shop just how much can be done with hand tools if they were available any longer. I am still looking for that spoke shave so I can make some replacement wagon wheels that I may need someday. I was able to make all the roof shingles with a device called a froe, which I found through a mail order catalogue. After the novelty of working with manual labor, myself, and hand tools wore off, I started milling lumber from the redwood logs I found in the winter creek bed using a chainsaw mill I setup. Money was still a bit scarce so I had to buy building materials a little at a time. The only reason I was even able to continue development of the property was because the labor was free and very energetic.

Early into the construction projects, several opportunities arose for me to go first to a private residence then an elementary school to remove as many materials as I could within two weeks prior to the structures being demolished for new development projects to go in. Free materials and free labor, I must be dreaming! The contractor's on each of the projects did not know who I was nor did they express any concern to me about their exposure in the event I was hurt while removing stuff, they just went on the word of our common contact that I was a responsible individual who knew what he was doing. Boy am I a salesman or what! I took as much time away from work as I could to relive the vision of 'when the lights went out in Newark' and get as much stuff out of these structures as I could before the demolition crews came in to relieve me. With the elementary school, I started in the principals office because I had a lot of issues to work out over past frustrations surrounding teaching and learning goals established by these institutions of lower learning caliber. The term 'it isn't my fault' may have originated in my mind about that time. Anyway I used it a lot because in 3rd or 4th grade it really isn't the kids fault for what happens. Anyway, I got so much reusable stuff out of the school like pink and blue slab doors, birch paneling, chalk boards, that I was set to now get serious with building our dream home going forward. Shortly after the school escapade I ended up scoring a whole bunch of interior trim and fixtures from the residence about to be demolished.

It took almost 25 years to fully complete the home, literally doing most of the work myself. Foundations were the hardest to do alone, while framing the structures least challenging and finish work the most time consuming but rewarding for me. At one point Sunset Magazine sent someone out to do an article on the workbench I built out of some of that birch wood from the principals office. As beautiful and functional as the workbench turned out, I think the reporter was more intrigued by the cable controlled tarp roof structure I designed to protect my tools and the bench with. Someone from Fine Homebuilding also approached me a little later on to do a cover article on several of the accessory structures I built by that time. I remember how intrigued the reporter was that came out from Fine Homebuilding, wondering how I built so much with such intricate detail in such rustic conditions. The elevator I designed and built to take us up to the second story bedroom of the cottage that we eventually moved over to from the treehouse, was one of the focal points in the article. The unisex urinal I designed in the bedroom allowed us not to disturb each other when going up and down on the elevator if we had to get up during the night to relieve ourselves. Later into the project we had saved enough money to have the final addition to the home built by a local contractor. Although I was very reluctant to have anyone else touch my creation up until now, in an effort to advance physically and mentally to the next stage in our lives, we had the addition completed up to rough framing and weather tight, at which point I took over for the next ten or so years to complete the finish work on the outside including making many of the exterior doors, stained glass windows and more gingerbread trim. I also, in my spare time, made many pieces of Victorian period furniture for the inside of the home.

Meanwhile, after about 6 years of pounding the pavement to try and convince Original Equipment Manufacturers to endorse media maintenance into their preventative hardware maintenance schedule, things really began to take off. Our process was never specifically endorsed by OEM's since they did not develop the procedure themselves, but the need to perform the maintenance function on removable disk packs that we did was recommended from that point on. With little competition in the beginning and no other vendors using our method of maintaining and preserving the integrity of the data on the devices, my client base quickly expanded. I would be in San Francisco working on a system while receiving a call that City of Eureka was having trouble retrieving data off one of their devices. Several days later I would find myself at the Sheriffs Office in Fresno or surrounded by a mountain of raw sugar at the C & H Sugar processing plant in Crockett, inspecting and cleaning their removable disk packs that usually had a faint odor of burnt sugar on them. I ended up going to so many interesting places of business during that career opportunity in addition to making a good living for my wife and I in the process.

Looking back, during that 25 plus years of my life I realize now that I essentially worked two full time jobs, non-stop, to reach my goal with attaining the American dream. I went on for another 10 years after that remodeling our next home extensively while exploring other career opportunities at the same time, in essence carrying on the tradition of a 70-80 hour work week schedule. My life has been enriched in so many ways that words can not describe my true feelings. Everything I have accomplished in life has such depth in meaning because I worked so very hard to discover for myself what lies behind the façade that most human beings never challenge themselves to explore for themselves. For people to hear something or have an idea and not pursue their dreams and ambitions past mere words or thoughts is so foreign to me personally that I just want to shake the whole bunch of you and just say 'try it you may like it.' "I can't even change a light bulb, I surely can't build anything myself," besides that's what you hire professionals to do! If you tell me that you don't like to get your hands dirty, I'm going to shake you again!

I understand with our current climate of fear and uncertainty in this country that people are reluctant to step out of their comfort zones, and lack the courage to try something new, but come on people! The thin air we are all breathing today is entirely man-made so that as we gasp for our next breath we feel powerless to do anything except try and survive, and that is exactly the position the rich and powerful want the majority of the good people of this nation to be in. When a persons ambitions are diminished and their hope for a better life is taken away, what is left but to go along with those in a position of power who can dictate what is in *your* best interest, since you are now too weak to make that choice yourself. If I had accepted the word of our government leaders in my youth, that the spread of communism must be stopped before reaching our shores, I may have never been able to explore my inner being while following the path to enlightenment as I did. Everyone can still work to attain the American dream of living an enriched and fulfilling life during the brief passage on this planet, but only if you desire to do so. If you could look into my mind to see what I have experienced in life so far, I guarantee you would be down at the hardware store tomorrow buying every power tool available to get started.

Working as hard as I did throughout my lifetime afforded me a few material benefits to enjoy now, but more than that the memory of how I got to where I am today is unique to me and shared by no other living creature on earth. That gift of enlightenment and understanding I now hold within is not a commodity even the most wealthy and powerful individual on the planet could obtain for themselves. And that feels pretty good, believe me! My parents always implied that I was different than the children around me. Well yeah! It wasn't my fault I was born in the nation of Texas. Never knowing what they meant, I now know what they were trying to say was that I was truly unique compared to my piers. And not to put words in their dear departed mouths, I like to think their belief was that I was 'special' among so many who are still searching for the meaning of life and their purpose on planet earth.

So that is a very condensed story of my life so far. I know I speak from higher ground than most people have ever experienced being on, but more than that I speak from the heart when I say believe in yourself, believe in your ability to overcome the obstacles placed before you day in and day out and always know you are the only true judge with what is in your own best interest to succeed and find purpose throughout you brief journey on this still glowing star in our universe.